Michael Frost has done it again, as he continues to raise the temperature for missional living. In *Surprise the World: The Five Habits of Highly Missional People*, Frost gives us a memorable strategy that we each can put into practice every day. You'll want to get multiple copies to share with your team to ensure that each one of us is prepared to live on mission to help even more people find their way back to God.

DAVE FERGUSON
Lead pastor of Community Christian Church

Even after people read multiple books, they often ask, "So what does being missional really look like?" One of my answers is to go practice Mike Frost's BELLS. Mike has simplified the way of Jesus for our world today. Grab some friends, commit, and watch the kingdom become tangible.

HUGH HALTER
Author of *Brimstone*, *Flesh*, and *The Tangible Kingdom*

Surprise the World is Mike Frost's missional genius made accessible for the average person. So many lives will change as a result, as people hear about and follow Jesus.

DAN KIMBALL
Pastor, Vintage Faith Church

Michael Frost's insights have made him a leading voice in the missional church movement. The habits commended in *Surprise the World* will only cement Michael's place as an original thinker who envisions and serves those of us who are pastors and leaders in churches. I will enthusiastically commend this book to the churches for whom I am bishop, and I will make use of it to train Holy Trinity Church, where I am pastor.

BISHOP TODD HUNTER
The Anglican Church in North America

A core part of the gospel is that Jesus came from the comfort of heaven to a dark and broken world in order to rescue humankind. If we're to see another awakening in America, Christ followers will need to be intentional about obeying the Great Commission to "go and make disciples." In *Surprise the World*, Michael Frost does an excellent job of explaining how to intentionally establish habits to share God's love with the people around us.

GERARD LONG
Founder, Awakening to Love Ministries

Christians should be different: We should challenge convention and stand out from culture. Too often we stand out for the wrong reasons. In *Surprise the World* Michael Frost challenges us to lead lives that cause the world to question how we love and serve so well. This book is a timely wake-up call for believers and a concise and helpful encouragement to those seeking to live on-mission in their communities. Mike is the real deal and so is this book!

ED STETZER
www.edstetzer.com

In this brief but powerful book, Michael suggests simple, missional practices that can be applied in any context. He maps a way forward that demonstrates how small gatherings of friends can help one another live into these practices. If every follower of Jesus developed a lifestyle that included these five habits, I'm convinced that a great spiritual awakening would take place in the neighborhoods, towns, and cities of our world.

AL ENGLER
Mission director, Nav Neighbors

Eminently doable, entirely practical, and exceptionally effective! In *Surprise the World*, renowned missiologist Michael Frost creates a compelling vision of what happens when a group of Jesus followers put into practice five proven habits of missional living. You want to see your community reached with the Good News? Get your church to read this outstanding book!

FELICITY DALE
Author of *An Army of Ordinary People*

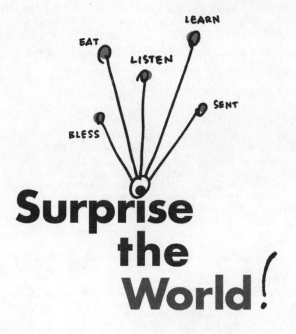

Surprise the World!

The Five Habits of Highly Missional People

MICHAEL FROST

A NavPress resource published in alliance
with Tyndale House Publishers, Inc.

NavPress is the publishing ministry of The Navigators, an international Christian organization and leader in personal spiritual development. NavPress is committed to helping people grow spiritually and enjoy lives of meaning and hope through personal and group resources that are biblically rooted, culturally relevant, and highly practical.

For more information, visit www.NavPress.com.

Surprise the World: The Five Habits of Highly Missional People

Copyright © 2016 by Michael Frost. All rights reserved.

A NavPress resource published in alliance with Tyndale House Publishers, Inc.

NAVPRESS and the NAVPRESS logo are registered trademarks of NavPress, The Navigators, Colorado Springs, CO. *TYNDALE* is a registered trademark of Tyndale House Publishers, Inc. Absence of ® in connection with marks of NavPress or other parties does not indicate an absence of registration of those marks.

Cover design by Jen Phelps

The Team:
Don Pape, Publisher
David Zimmerman, Acquiring Editor, Development Editor, Copyeditor

All Scripture quotations, unless otherwise marked, are taken from the Holy Bible, *New International Version,*® *NIV.*® Copyright © 1973, 1978, 1984, 2011 by Biblica, Inc.® Used by permission. All rights reserved worldwide.

Scripture quotations marked ESV are taken from *The Holy Bible*, English Standard Version® (ESV®), copyright © 2001 by Crossway, a publishing ministry of Good News Publishers. Used by permission. All rights reserved.

Some of the anecdotal illustrations in this book are true to life and are included with the permission of the persons involved. All other illustrations are composites of real situations, and any resemblance to people living or dead is coincidental.

Library of Congress Cataloging-in-Publication Data

Frost, Michael, date.
  Surprise the world : the five habits of highly missional people / Michael Frost.
    pages cm
  ISBN 978-1-63146-516-1
1. Missions. 2. Evangelistic work. 3. Witness bearing (Christianity) I. Title.
  BV2063.F76 2016
  266—dc23   2015033534

Printed in the United States of America

22   21   20   19   18   17
11   10   9   8   7

CONTENTS

INTRODUCTION

I really didn't set out to create an international movement. When I came up with the BELLS model described in this book, I thought it was just a simple idea our church could adopt to foster missional habits in our lives. I had no idea that churches right across the world—the United States, Canada, the United Kingdom, New Zealand, and goodness knows where else—would embrace it. But now it seems that everywhere I go I meet folks who tell me they are living out these five simple habits in an attempt to better fulfill the mission of God.

I partly blame my good friend Alan Hirsch. He regularly mentions BELLS in his lectures and seminars as an example of how churches can encourage missional living within their members. Although I have outlined the model in a couple of my earlier books, I have tended to be more coy about BELLS, preferring to encourage churches to create their own homegrown approach to missional living rather than expecting them to simply adopt our model.

But when recently the folks at the Exponential church-planting movement asked me to write a manual on how to do BELLS, I figured it was time to abandon my diffidence and go ahead and fly the flag. So the book you're holding was originally an e-book posted on the Exponential site. I was delighted when NavPress then expressed interest in offering it in a paper-and-ink format, and set about expanding the simple format into a more detailed explanation of the BELLS habits and how they can work in fostering a missional lifestyle. I suspect the reason why people have embraced BELLS so quickly is that it's such a simple, easy-to-adopt set of habits that do unleash essential missional values: engagement with neighbors, connection with each other, a deeper experience of God's leading, a stronger understanding of the gospel, and a framework for identifying ourselves as missionaries. (I include a tracking sheet for these habits in the final chapter of the book.)

I'm not suggesting that BELLS is a magic bullet or anything like that. But it is a really handy tool for mobilizing Christians up, in, and out into mission. That is, *up* into deeper connection with the Triune God; *in* to a stronger sense of community with other believers; and *out* into the neighborhood.

The fact is that we all recognize the need to live generous, hospitable, Spirit-led, Christlike lives as missionaries to our own neighborhoods. We want to live our faith out in the open for all to see.

Unfortunately, some of us grew up in churches that expected something less from us. For a start, we were often told we are all evangelists, and we were expected to memorize prefabricated gospel presentations and to go forth and share that presentation with anyone who would listen. For a lot of us this was a mortifying prospect. For a variety of reasons (temperament, lack of knowledge, lack of relationship), we felt inadequate to do so, and we ended up feeling guilty about our lack of evangelistic zeal. Often, those who were confident enough to do it were so obnoxious in their approach that they turned unbelievers away in droves.

Even when we felt released from the burden of having to be gung-ho evangelists, we still got the impression that all we had to do was befriend our neighbors and colleagues and invite them to church to hear the preaching of the Word.

I have no doubt that some people have become Christians by being buttonholed by a wild-eyed evangelist with a tract or by being invited to church by a Christian neighbor. But I think both approaches are unfair to us. The former places too high a set of expectations on us—after all, not everyone is a gifted evangelist. But the latter reduces us to church marketers whose primary role is to advertise the church's benefits.

Surely there is a way we can see the church as "an army of ordinary people,"[1] sent out to announce and demonstrate the reign of God through Christ, without expecting ourselves to be something we're not or something less than we should be.

That's where BELLS comes in. I believe the key to equip believers to see themselves as "sent ones," to foster a series of missional habits that shape our lives and values, and to propel us into the world confidently and filled with hope. These are the five habits of highly missional people.

Living "Questionable" Lives

Before we get to the five habits themselves, allow me to sketch the background. Evangelistic mission works effectively when we are living generous, hospitable, Spirit-led, Christlike lives as missionaries to our own neighborhoods—*and* when the gifted evangelists in our midst join us in sharing Christ with our neighbors. That's not just good evangelism strategy. That's the biblical model.

A Twofold Approach to Evangelism

With all the best intentions in the world, some people will tell you that every Christian is an evangelist and bears the responsibility to share Christ with others.

I certainly agree with the latter part of that contention (that we bear responsibility to share our love for Jesus with others). But I fear that the first part of that statement (that every Christian is an evangelist) is unhelpful.

Are we really all evangelists? Certainly the vast majority of Christians I know don't feel much like evangelists. It's as if we're being told that—even though we don't believe we're evangelists, and don't perform very effectively when we act like evangelists—we are nonetheless, deep down in our bones, really truly evangelists who just need to step into our true identities and fulfill our calling to share Christ with others. Is this fair, and more importantly, is it true?

Contrary to the myth that every believer is an evangelist, the apostle Paul assumes a twofold approach to the ministry of evangelism.

- First, he affirms the gifting of the evangelist— interestingly, not the gift of evangel*ism* but the evangelist herself is the gift (see Ephesians 4:11).
- Second, he writes as though all believers are to be evangelistic in their general orientation.

Paul clearly places himself in the first category, seeing his ministry not only as that of an apostle but also as that of an evangelist. But it doesn't appear that he believes *all* Christians bear the responsibility for the kind of bold proclamation to which he is called. Note his description of this twofold approach in his letter to the Colossians:

> Devote yourselves to prayer, being watchful and thankful. And pray for us, too, that God may open a door for our message, so that we may proclaim the mystery of Christ, for which I am in chains. Pray that I may proclaim it clearly, as I should. Be wise in the way you act toward outsiders; make the most of every opportunity. Let your conversation be always full of grace, seasoned with salt, so that you may know how to answer everyone.
>
> COLOSSIANS 4:2-6

For evangelists, Paul asks for opportunities to share Christ and for the courage to proclaim the gospel clearly (verses 3-4). But he doesn't suggest the Colossians pray as much for themselves. Rather, evangelistic believers are to pray for the evangelists' ministry, to be wise in their conduct toward outsiders, and to look for opportunities to answer outsiders' questions when they arise (verses 2, 5-6). When it comes to the spoken aspect of their ministries, evangelists are to proclaim, and believers are to give answers.

Type of Minister	Priorities	Type of Spoken Ministry
Gifted Evangelists	Clarity in the Gospel; Alertness for Opportunities	Bold Proclamation
Evangelistic Believers	Prayer, Watchfulness, Wise Socializing	Gracious Answers

Paul's twofold approach to evangelism in the church

I think Paul assumed that the number of gifted evangelists wouldn't be great. It seems clear that he thinks the gifted evangelists can be local (like Timothy—see 2 Timothy 4:5) or translocal (like himself). He seems also to have assumed that some gifted evangelists would occupy a leadership function in local churches (see Ephesians 4:11), building up the church to be increasingly evangelistic.

While evangelism is an essential gifting for all churches,

it isn't a gifting given to every believer. Believers, as noted, were to pray like crazy and to conduct themselves, in word and deed, in such a way as to provoke unbelievers to question their beliefs and enter into an evangelistic dialogue. On this Peter is in agreement with Paul:

> Always be prepared to give an answer to
> everyone who asks you to give the reason
> for the hope that you have. But do this
> with gentleness and respect, keeping a clear
> conscience, so that those who speak maliciously
> against your good behavior in Christ may be
> ashamed of their slander.
>
> 1 PETER 3:15-16

In other words, the biblical model is for leaders to (1) identify, equip, and mobilize gifted evangelists (who then take a leadership responsibility for the church's evangelism) and (2) inspire all believers to *live questionable lives*. If all believers are leading the kinds of lives that evoke questions from their friends, then opportunities for sharing faith abound, and chances for the gifted evangelists to boldly proclaim are increased. In brief, our task is to surprise the world!

Some evangelists have taken me to task for teaching this biblical model. They fear I am letting people off the hook when it comes to evangelism. I have been told by more than one gifted evangelist that telling people they're not required to create opportunities for bold evangelistic proclamation means that people will never tell others about Jesus. I disagree. I think gifted evangelistic *leaders* bear the responsibility to *equip* their congregations to be able to tell others about Jesus, but the opportunities for faith sharing will emerge *from questioning unbelievers*. Gifted evangelistic leaders should be training their congregations to speak about Jesus conversationally when questioned about how they deal with suffering, or why they spend their vacation serving the poor, or why they've opened their home to refugees, or why they're fasting during Lent, or why they've made career choices that allow them to contribute to the greater social good.

The fact is, gifted evangelists telling the rest of us that we should behave like gifted evangelists has a debilitating effect. We look at confident, articulate, theologically trained evangelists preaching in our churches, and we hear their stories of sharing the gospel on the back of a napkin in a restaurant or a plane, and then we hear them tell us that we, too, can (and indeed, should) do what they do—and we freeze! We know we can't do what they do.

But I don't hear Paul telling his congregations to preach in the Areopagus like he did. He doesn't berate them for not creating opportunities for bold, clear proclamation. He *does* want them to talk about Jesus, but as we've seen, he assumes it should be in the context of wise socializing, prompted by the questions of others.

Taking Over the Empire

This twofold approach literally transformed the Roman Empire. While evangelists and apologists such as Peter and Paul were proclaiming the gospel and defending its integrity in an era of polytheism and pagan superstition, hundreds of thousands of ordinary believers were infiltrating every part of society and living the kind of questionable lives that evoked curiosity about the Christian message. They surprised the empire with their unlikely lifestyle.

These ordinary believers devoted themselves to sacrificial acts of kindness. They loved their enemies and forgave their persecutors. They cared for the poor and fed the hungry. In the brutality of life under Roman rule, they were the most stunningly different people anyone had ever seen. Indeed, their influence was so surprising that the fourth-century emperor Julian (AD 331–363) feared they might take over the empire. Referring to Christians as "Galileans" and Christianity as "atheism" (because of their denial of the existence of pagan gods) and believing their religion to be a sickness, he penned this directive to his officials:

> We must pay special attention to this point, and by this means effect a cure. For when it came about that the poor were neglected and overlooked by the [pagan] priests, then I think the impious Galileans observed this fact and devoted themselves to philanthropy. And they have gained ascendancy in the worst of their deeds through the credit they win for such practices. For just as those who entice children with a cake, and by throwing it to them two or three times induce them to follow them, and then, when they are far away from their friends cast them on board a ship and sell them

as slaves . . . by the same method, I say, the
Galileans also begin with their so-called love-
feast, or hospitality, or service of tables—for
they have many ways of carrying it out and
hence call it by many names—and the result
is that they have led very many into atheism
[i.e., Christianity].[1]

Julian was concerned that the Christians' acts of hospitality and philanthropy were winning too many of
his subjects. He decided to launch an offensive against
them by mobilizing his officials and the pagan priest-
hood to *out-love* the Christians. He decreed that a system of food distribution be started and that hostels be
built for poor travelers:

Why do we not observe that it is their
benevolence to strangers, their care for the
graves of the dead and the pretended holiness
of their lives that have done most to increase
atheism? I believe that we ought really and
truly to practice every one of these virtues. . . .
For it is disgraceful that when . . . the impious
Galileans support not only their own poor but

ours as well, all men see that our people lack
aid from us.[2]

Perhaps not surprisingly, Julian's new social program
utterly failed. He couldn't motivate pagan priests or
Roman officials to care that much for the poor. He
failed to realize that the Christians were filled with the
Holy Spirit of love and motivated by his grace. The
message they shared—that God loved the world—was
patently absurd to the average Roman; the pagan gods
cared nothing for humankind. And yet in the miserable
world of the Roman Empire, the Christians not only
proclaimed the mercy of God but also demonstrated it.
They not only fed the poor; they welcomed all comers,
regardless of their socioeconomic status. The nobleman
embraced the slave. Moreover, Christians opened their
fellowship to anyone irrespective of ethnicity, and they
promoted social relations between the sexes and within
families. They were literally the most surprising alternative society, and their conduct raised an insatiable
curiosity among the average Roman.

You can see how the proclamation of gifted evangelists would have been far more effective among a society
of people living such questionable lives. I think this is

what Paul referred to as "adorning" the gospel—or in more contemporary language, making the gospel attractive. He uses this phrase when exhorting Titus to teach sound doctrine:

> You, however, must teach what is appropriate to sound doctrine. Teach the older men to be temperate, worthy of respect, self-controlled, and sound in faith, in love and in endurance.
>
> Likewise, teach the older women to be reverent in the way they live, not to be slanderers or addicted to much wine, but to teach what is good. Then they can urge the younger women to love their husbands and children, to be self-controlled and pure, to be busy at home, to be kind, and to be subject to their husbands, so that no one will malign the word of God.
>
> Similarly, encourage the young men to be self-controlled. In everything set them an example by doing what is good. In your teaching show integrity, seriousness and soundness of speech that cannot be condemned, so that those who oppose you

may be ashamed because they have nothing
bad to say about us.

Teach slaves to be subject to their masters
in everything, to try to please them, not to talk
back to them, and not to steal from them, but
to show that they can be fully trusted, so that
in every way they will make the teaching about
God our Savior attractive.

TITUS 2:1-10

Note the way Paul concludes this list of rules (verse
10). He does not tell Titus to teach his congregation
of slaves and free, young and old, to conduct themselves in this manner in order to win God's mercy—that
mercy is offered freely in God our Savior. Instead, Paul
insists that Christians live this way in order to "make
the teaching of the church attractive."

Nothing would be more questionable in the first
century than a slave who loved his master, or a self-
controlled young man, or an old woman who didn't
engage in slander. In other words, this was Paul's recipe
for a questionable life in his time. Our challenge is to
find what similarly questionable lives look like in the
twenty-first century.

What Kind of Life Will Evoke Questions?

There's an old communication theory that goes like this: When predictability is high, impact is low. In other words, when the audience thinks they know what you're going to say, and you go ahead and say it, it makes very little impact. On the other hand, when an audience is surprised or intrigued, they will think long and hard about what they've heard.

The same goes for Christian outreach. Remember that one of the primary acts of the evangelistic believer is the arousal of curiosity among unbelievers, leading to questions and faith sharing. Acts of philanthropy by Christians today are relatively commonplace, so they don't surprise the world. If we hear that a Christian business owner has donated money to a cause, or that a church has opened a feeding program or a hospice, we aren't intrigued. Such things are expected. I'm not suggesting Christian philanthropy shouldn't continue as an expression of the grace offered to us in Christ, but it doesn't evoke questions the way it might have in the fourth century.

Neither does living a fine, upstanding, middle-class lifestyle in the suburbs, for what it's worth. Again, I'm not saying we ought not to live our lives this way. But if we're trying to live questionable lives, then cutting the lawn, saying hi to the neighbors, washing our car, walking the dog, and driving to the office every day is hardly an intriguing lifestyle.

To fulfill the evangelistic mandate that Paul and Peter and the gospel present us with, we need to be propelled *outward*, into the lives of our neighbors, but also *upward*, into deeper intimacy with Jesus. This isn't merely an individual challenge; indeed, Paul seems to suggest that we fulfill our evangelistic mandate collectively, as we also move *inward* into a self-consciously Christian community, acknowledging the evangelists we've been gifted with and the responsibility to live questionable lives that we've been vested with. We need to become a godly, intriguing, socially adventurous, joyous presence in the lives of others.

This won't be a matter of simply doing somewhat surprising but occasional things. I believe we need to develop a new set of rhythms, or habits, that foster a missional lifestyle that intrigues others. And I think the five habits I'm about to unpack will help you to do that.

→ *Reflect on the rhythms of your life. Which of them are motivated primarily by your faith?*

→ *Of those, which do you think would qualify as "questionable"—practices that the non-Christians in your life would find surprising or intriguing?*

②

A New Set of Habits

We're all used to our churches launching short-term or one-off initiatives to get us out into our neighborhoods, sharing our lives and faith with others (for example, 40 Days of Purpose, connection weeks, Serve the City weekends). I don't decry the impact of such concerted efforts. But what I'm addressing here is something different: the challenge of finding regular rhythms or habits that transform our everyday lifestyles.

The links between our (inner) spirituality and our (outward) action are far greater than many believe. In fact, Jesus and the New Testament writers saw a powerful integration of faith and action, so much so that they found it impossible to separate them. In fact, to separate a person from his or her actions can be very dangerous. The apostle James says, "Show me your faith without deeds, and I will show you my faith by my deeds" (James 2:18). It is far more biblical to see action as a powerful expression of the person who takes that action. Indeed, Swiss psychiatrist Carl Jung once said, "You are what you do, not what you say you'll do."

Whereas we often see our faith being exhibited in action, there's also a strong case to be made for suggesting it can flow in the other direction, too. That is, our actions can shape our faith. As Aristotle said, "We are what we repeatedly do. Excellence, then, is not an act, but a habit."

Transfer that idea to faith. Faith, then, is not an act, a single choice, or even just a belief system; it is a *habit*.

French philosopher Pierre Bourdieu referred to this as *habitus*. In his view, society at large develops a complex series of norms, tendencies that guide the behavior and thinking of its members. In other words, the practices and actions that a society endorses in turn shape the way members of that society think. Habitus is the way a society helps people to think, feel, and act in determinantal ways, which then guide them.

For example, the majority of Americans would have the view that getting married, building a career, buying a house, and raising a family are important and desirable milestones. These are examples of an American habitus. They are desirable practices (or habits, if you will), which in turn reinforce a belief system that values monogamy, homeownership, professionalism, consumerism, and reproduction. Of course, not every American values these things or desires these practices. And plenty of those who do value these things don't necessarily live them out perfectly. But they are expected societal practices that in turn shape core American values. In this sense habitus is created and reproduced unconsciously, without any deliberate pursuit of consistency.

Just as a society's desirable habits shape that society's values, so can an individual's personal habits shape his or her values. In fact, I think this is a much-overlooked aspect of discipleship. We need to be fostering a set of habits among Christians that will in turn shape their values and beliefs. That's what BELLS is; more on that to come.

There was once a time when evangelicals saw a daily "quiet time" as an essential habit for nurturing their faith. Today it seems to have gone by the wayside, but at its best it was a daily rhythm that fostered a love for the Bible and prayer. Now, try to imagine how the "quiet time" came to be so essential to our parents and grandparents. No doubt, Bible study and prayer have always been important values to Christians, but over time they took the shape of a daily routine that included the reading of short sections of Scripture and a brief reflection on its meaning, followed by prayers for needs and concerns. Soon, Christian agencies were producing booklets aimed at facilitating this endeavor. Eventually, church leaders didn't so much need to promote Bible reading and prayer per se. Instead they promoted the importance of having a daily "quiet time," and they distributed the booklets and tools to facilitate it. The habit had taken effect. And the habit deepened the value it was created to foster.

This leads me back to my earlier question about what might so surprise our friends that they would question our motivations and provide us opportunities to talk with them about Jesus. I think the answer has something to do with the kind of missional habits we adopt.

Missional Habits

Sometimes called "missional rhythms" or "missional practices," missional habits are those habits we foster in our lives that, in turn, shape our missional outlook.

By *missional*, I mean all that we do and say that alerts others to the reign of God.

South African missiologist David Bosch wrote, "Mission is more than and different from recruitment to our brand of religion; it is the alerting of people to the universal reign of God through Christ."[1] In other words, mission derives from the reign of God. In that respect, the ideas of our mission and God's kingdom are irrevocably linked. Mission is both the announcement and the demonstration of the reign of God through Christ.

Mission is not primarily concerned with church growth. It is primarily concerned with the reign and rule of the Triune God. That is why those of us who are not gifted evangelists need to foster habits in our lives that draw us out into the lives of unbelievers and invite the kinds of questions that lead to evangelistic sharing. When our lives become questionable, our neighbors invite us to proclaim the reign of God. If the church grows as a result, so be it.

Missional habits aren't just strategic, they're consequential: Because of the universal reign of God through Christ, we bless, we open our tables, we listen for the Spirit, we learn Christ, and we are sent out on this evangelistic task. That being said, if our only habits as Christians are going to church and attending meetings, they're not going to connect us with unbelievers nor invite their curiosity about our faith.

The trick is to develop habits that unite us together as believers, while also propelling us into the lives of others. We also need habitual practices that don't deplete our energy and burn us out, but rather reenergize us, replenishing our reserves and connecting us more deeply to Jesus. I have seen these missional habits do just that.

BLESS	I will bless three people this week, at least one of whom is not a member of our church.
EAT	I will eat with three people this week, at least one of whom is not a member of our church.
LISTEN	I will spend at least one period of the week listening for the Spirit's voice.
LEARN	I will spend at least one period of the week learning Christ.
SENT	I will journal throughout the week about all the ways I alerted others to the universal reign of God through Christ.

BELLS: The five habits of highly missional people

I will explain more fully what is involved in each of these habits in the following chapters, but let me make the point here that each habit is designed to release a certain value in the life of the person who practices them.

- If you bless three people every week, you're going to become a very generous person.
- If you eat with others, you'll develop a greater capacity for hospitality.
- If you foster the habit of listening to the Holy Spirit, you'll become an increasingly Spirit-led person.
- If you're learning Christ, it's fair to assume you'll become more and more Christlike.
- If you're journaling the myriad ways you've been sent into your world, you'll increasingly see yourself as a sent one, or a missionary in your own neighborhood.

In other words, each habit shapes us around a particular missional value.

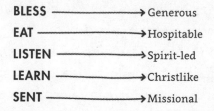

BLESS	⟶	Generous
EAT	⟶	Hospitable
LISTEN	⟶	Spirit-led
LEARN	⟶	Christlike
SENT	⟶	Missional

Missional habits and their missional values

My point is this: If you want to be a generous, hospitable, Spirit-led, Christlike missionary, don't just try to learn those values—foster these habits! Indeed, I'm pretty certain most churches have a mission or vision statement that says they are committed to something similar to this. I also suspect that most members of churches read these and agree with them in theory. But many people have very little idea of what exactly it means to live out these habits under the noses of those who have not yet been set free in Christ. To pastors I say, you don't have to preach these values if you're fostering the habits. The habits will in turn unleash the values naturally.

While I'm addressing pastors, allow me to say that I know a lot of you are interested in how to manage change in your churches. Much has been written about the highly turbulent time in which we live. Culture is changing rapidly. Church leaders invest a lot of time trying to figure out how to help their churches embrace the necessary changes in order to engage the world around them. Changing the behavior of people is a profoundly important challenge for churches trying to thrive in a shifting cultural environment. John Kotter, a Harvard Business School professor, says that "the central issue is never strategy, structure, culture, or systems. The core of the matter is always about changing the behavior of people."[2] Plowing a lot of energy into changing church structures, designing vision statements, teaching values, and fashioning strategies can be wasted unless people have some clear understanding of what *actual* behaviors are required. Pastor and scholar Lee Beach says,

> The temptation and often the pressure on church leaders is to always be devising a new evangelistic strategy or promoting the latest program that is working in other settings. This is not wrong in itself; in fact, evangelistic strategy can be part of missional effectiveness. However, it is not the core idea of mission in 1 Peter (or the New Testament as a whole). Peter's instruction to the church is that faithful evangelistic witness comes in the form of the simple, daily obedience of Christian people living together in authentic community and going into their world as ambassadors for Christ.[3]

The Shadow Side of Habitus

Of course, behavior change involves the challenge of familiarization. While a habit might deepen the value it was created to foster, it can also build up resistance to the potency of the habit. That's why drug users up their usage. Familiarization explains (at least partly) why the quiet time seems to have gone by the wayside. A habit that can't be named and claimed, so to speak, risks becoming rote and easier to abandon. This is the shadow side of habitus. It is the gap between ritual and revival.

Also, in the process of entrenching new values, habits can leave some values behind. The quiet time prioritized personal Bible reading and prayer, but it also privatized Christian practice, rendering social-gospel priorities, for example, as suspect because the dots don't easily connect between social engagement and personal/private disciplines.

The key is to develop *mindful* habits for all Christians so that their habitual practices don't become merely unconscious habits, like biting your nails. They should become a regular, everyday way of life, but we mustn't lose sight of the values they were designed to unleash. There are three ways I think missional habits can resist familiarization.

First, we should not forget the essential role of those gifted evangelistic leaders I spoke about in the previous chapter. It is their job not only to be evangelists but also to continue to equip us to share our faith and to remind us of the ultimate purpose of the habits we embrace. While I might find myself falling into mindlessly living out certain habits by rote, my gifted evangelistic leader should continually be fanning into flame a mindful awareness of the purpose behind those habits. This is why Paul's twofold approach is so strategic: We need both gifted evangelists and ordinary believers who are habitually evangelistic.

Second, we should remember that these are *missional* habits. They are designed to propel us outward, beyond ourselves, into the lives of others. While a very private experience such as a daily quiet time might easily become a ritual, the highly relational habits of blessing others, of practicing hospitality, and of seeing oneself as a sent one bring with them their own set of external accountabilities. If it is our habit to eat with unbelievers every week, the interaction with those unbelieving friends will serve to remind us of the reason for the habit in the first place.

Third, as I'll explain more fully later in this book,

we need to develop accountability relationships around us that not only ensure we commit to the habits but also help us see that missional living doesn't only arouse questions from others—it is also a great framework for our own deeper Christian discipleship as well.

→ *Reflect on habits you've developed that are related to your Christian faith. To what extent have these practices become familiarized to the point of being rote or routine?*

→ *In what ways might these habits more consistently propel you upward, inward, or outward as expressions of the reign and rule of God?*

③

Bless: The First Habit

I will bless three people this week—at least one of whom is not a member of our church.

The first habit I want you to consider embracing is that of blessing others. In fact, I'd like you to bless three people each week—at least one of whom is a member of your church and at least one of whom is *not.* The third can be from either category.

The term "to bless" can have various meanings. Technically, it describes the act of consecrating something or someone by religious rite or word. From the Old English *bletsian*, which was in turn from the Proto-Germanic *blodison*, it originally meant "to hallow by the sprinkling of blood on pagan altars."

When the Bible was being translated into Old English, the term was chosen to translate the Latin *benedicere* and Greek *eulogein*, both of which have the meaning "to speak well of; to praise." Later, the meaning shifted toward "to pronounce or make happy."

Today, Christians use the word *bless* in a variety of ways. In most respects it means to confer prosperity or happiness upon another. Even blessing someone who has just sneezed is an expression of such goodwill and a desire for continued health.

I've heard that part of the etymology of the term "to bless" is "to add strength to another's arm." In this respect, to bless others is to build them up, to fill them with encouragement for them to increase in strength and prosperity.

(Incidentally, I know Christians often talk about "blessing God," and since it's impossible for us to add strength to God's arm, it seems an odd use of the term. The reason for it, though, is that the Old English *bletsian* was also chosen to translate the Hebrew *brk*, which meant "to bend the knee, worship, praise, invoke blessings"—an entirely appropriate reference to our relationship to God.)

What does it mean to add strength to another's arm? Anything that relieves their burden in life. Anything that helps them breathe more easily. Anything that lifts their spirit or alleviates their distress. It can be a small thing or large. From my experience, blessing another generally takes three different forms.

Words of Affirmation

Words of affirmation are the simplest way to bless someone. Send them a note, write them an e-mail, or text them. Send them some words of affirmation and encouragement. Let them know you've noticed something worthwhile about them. Mark Twain once said, "I can live for two months on a good compliment." I've heard it said that a word of encouragement is like oxygen to the soul. Beautiful. A word of affirmation helps our souls to breathe more easily.

Gary Chapman includes words of affirmation as one of his five love languages; he describes them as verbal support to communicate love. But he goes further. He identifies the importance of empathy in blessing others with words of affirmation:

> Encouragement requires empathy and seeing the world from [another's] perspective. We must first learn what is important to [the other]. Only

then can we give encouragement. With verbal encouragement, we are trying to communicate, "I know. I care. I am with you. How can I help?" We are trying to show that we believe in [the person] and in [his or her] abilities. We are giving credit and praise.[1]

Acts of Kindness

Who doesn't feel blessed when someone does them a favor or provides some kind of practical support? Cutting an old lady's lawn. Babysitting an exhausted couple's kids. Helping a neighbor move to his new house. These acts of kindness literally add strength to their arm; they lighten the recipient's load. Look for ways to perform an act of kindness in someone's life.

I have an old Alcoholics Anonymous "Just For Today" card which contains nine daily promises a recovering alcoholic is required to make as part of the program. The fifth promise is "I will do somebody a good turn and will not get found out. If anybody knows of it, it will not count." That's nice, isn't it? I'm not suggesting you have to perform secret acts of kindness as the AA program recommends, but it's the same principle. Exercise your soul and bless others by doing them a good turn this week. It will not only bless your soul but will also provide practical assistance to another and hopefully, over time, deepen your bonds with each other.

Gifts

The recipient of a gift thrives on the love, thoughtfulness, and effort behind the gift. A gift can show the recipient that he or she is known, cared for, and valued. And I'm not just talking about birthday or Christmas gifts. I mean totally random gift giving. Almost everything ever written on the subject of love indicates that at the heart of love is the spirit of giving. A gift is a symbol of that thought.

Gifts come in all sizes, colors, and shapes. Some are expensive, and others are free. Some gifts are given for obvious reasons—a struggling single mother would appreciate a food basket, while the victim of some misfortune would value being cheered up. But some gifts are nothing more than an expression that the recipient has been thought of.

Remember, I want you to bless at least one member of your church and one person who is not a Christian.

This means the blessing ricochets around your church, as members are affirming, gifting, and performing acts of kindness for each other. It also means church members are propelled outward to bless unbelievers in these ways. Just watch how unleashing a culture of blessing—words of affirmation, acts of kindness, gift giving—binds people to each other. It has the effect of strengthening the Christian community while launching its members more deeply into the lives of outsiders.

Even more than that, the simple act of blessing can have huge evangelistic impact as well. In his book *Discover Your Mission Now*, Dave Ferguson recounts reading a doctoral thesis entitled *Blessers Versus Converters*. The researcher had looked at two teams of short-term missionaries that visited Thailand with distinctly different missional strategies. The team referred to as the "blessers" went with the intention of simply blessing people. They saw their mission as being to bless whomever came their way in whatever practical ways they could. The "converters," on the other hand, went with the sole intention of converting people and evangelizing everyone they encountered.

The research found, perhaps unsurprisingly, that the blessers had far greater social impact. That makes sense.

When short-term missionaries go with the intention of contributing to the social good of their context, their social impact will be high. But Ferguson points out a second finding:

> Secondly, and here is what was so surprising, they discovered that the "blessers" also had almost 50 times as many conversions than the "converters"! The "blessers" were 50 times more successful at helping people find their way back to God![2]

This would surely be because of the point made earlier: When we live unexpected lives (which clearly includes blessing strangers), we find ourselves being questioned by others. Then we have the best opportunity for sharing the hope of Christ within us.

A Few Words of Caution about Blessing

Having said all that, let me sound a few words of caution. First, while blessing others will certainly provide opportunities to share your faith with them, we need to be watchful that we're not being generous friends *merely* in order to convert them. We are called to bless in order to bless, because we were made to bless the nations. No doubt those fourth-century Christians that Emperor Julian was complaining about were feeding the poor, ministering to the dying, and practicing benevolence toward plenty of strangers who didn't convert. It wasn't an evangelistic strategy, as such. It was simply their guileless lifestyle. And it was habitual. This was the source of Julian's outrage: The Galileans, as he called them, were doing these things with no sense of personal gain in mind. We need to develop a rhythm of gift giving, time spending, and affirmation sharing as an end in itself because it fosters a spirit of generosity, it mirrors the character of God, and it alerts others to his reign.

The second word of caution is to remind you that the key to successful blessing is that the recipient must *feel blessed*. Remember, our action ought to add strength to their arm. If people feel manipulated or used by our blessings, those blessings can hardly be considered as such. Giving gifts in order to get a return from someone (like bribing people to attend our churches) leaves a nasty taste in people's mouths. Keep Paul's words in Philippians 2:3-4 in mind:

Do nothing out of selfish ambition or vain
conceit. Rather, in humility value others above
yourselves, not looking to your own interests
but each of you to the interests of the others.

Even if no one asks us about our motivations, we
resolve to live out a habitual rhythm of gift giving,
time spending, and affirmation sharing. We will be
humble, gentle, loving, and consistent. Bear in mind
the proverb, "If anyone loudly blesses their neighbor early in the morning, it will be taken as a curse"
(Proverbs 27:14). The act of blessing must be consid-
erate to achieve its purpose.

All this implies that blessers must become students
of those whom they bless. We must become attentive
to the needs, fears, hopes, and yearnings of our neighbors in order to bless them appropriately. Church
history is full of stories in which whole nations were
colonized by "Christian" empires; colonial-era missionaries thought they were bringing a blessing to the
locals, but in fact they were seen as part of the ter-
ror and dehumanization inflicted upon these indig-
enous cultures. The founding father of Kenya, Jomo
Kenyatta, was noted as saying, "When the missionaries

arrived, the Africans had the land and the missionaries had the Bible. They taught us how to pray with our eyes closed. When we opened them, they had the land and we had the Bible."[3] Whether that's an oversimplification or not, the fact is that the blessing of the Bible was not perceived as such by those who linked it entirely to the evils of colonization. Likewise, we can come across as "colonizers" in our neighborhoods if we're seen as the ones who only bless others if there's something in it for us.

But my third word of caution should be held in tension with what I've just said. While we do need to craft our blessings in a way that adds strength to the arm of those we bless, there's no guarantee that people won't misunderstand our motives or indeed hate us for our faith. Earlier, I quoted 1 Peter 3:15-16:

Always be prepared to give an answer to everyone who asks you to give the reason for the hope that you have. But do this with gentleness and respect, keeping a clear conscience, so that *those who speak maliciously against your good behavior in Christ* may be ashamed of their slander. [italics added]

Peter here insists we behave with gentleness and respect toward others, but he's under no illusions that this means people won't speak maliciously of us. Indeed, he may be recalling the words of Jesus in Matthew 5:11: "Blessed are you when people insult you, persecute you and falsely say all kinds of evil against you because of me."

The key, it seems, is to keep a clear conscience. If people revile us because of Christ, even though we've conducted ourselves toward them with humility, gentleness, and generosity, then so be it. Jesus promised it, after all. But if people revile us because we are manipulative jerks, that's on us.

→ *Bless three people this week—at least one of whom is not a member of your church.*

Eat: The Second Habit

I will eat with three people this week—at least one of whom is not a member of our church.

Back to cranky old Emperor Julian. Remember that one of his pet peeves about the Christians was their practice of a surprising form of hospitality. He complained to his officials that one of the Christians' methods for "perverting" the empire was their so-called love-feast, or service of tables. He appeared to be uncertain of the name of their gathering because, he said, "they have many ways of carrying it out and hence call it by many names."

So what was he referring to exactly? And how many different ways were there of carrying it out? Well, to begin with, it is doubtful that he was referring exclusively to the Eucharist or the practice of the Lord's Supper, although this was probably part of the original

Christian love-feasts. We know the Corinthians were practicing a communal meal as part of their weekly habit because Paul rebukes them for conducting it so poorly in 1 Corinthians 11:17-34. More on that later. In any case, it seems that the early Christians must have focused so much of their lifestyle and ministry around the table that outside observers like Julian were confused as to the exact nature of any given meal.

Around AD 112 Pliny the Younger, the Roman governor of Bithynia-Pontus (now in modern Turkey), wrote a letter to Emperor Trajan to ask for counsel on dealing with the church. He reported that the Christians would meet "on a fixed day" in the early morning to "sing responsively to Christ, as to a god." Later in the same day they would "assemble again to partake of food—but ordinary and innocent food."[1]

In other documents of the time, there appear various references to the separation of the Eucharist from the love feast, as though they were seen as two very distinct gatherings. This might be why Emperor Julian had trouble keeping track. In any case, a rhythm eventually developed where it was standard practice for the early Christians to celebrate the Eucharist in the morning and the love-feast in the evening.

My point is that eating has been a central Christian practice since the beginning of our movement. And not only eating sacramentally, as in the Eucharist, but eating missionally as a way to express love to all. More than that, eating with others can be perceived as a profoundly *theological* practice. It mirrors the character of the Triune God. As Janice Price of the Church of England World Mission Panel says,

> Hospitality, as the mutual indwelling one
> with another, becomes the modus operandi of
> mission as those in common participation in
> the life and mission of God meet and receive
> from each other. . . . Hospitality is an attitude
> of the heart which is about openness to the
> other. . . . This mirrors the hospitality of the
> Trinity as God chooses to open himself to
> the other through the Incarnation and to subject
> himself to the created order. . . . It is about a
> generous acknowledgement and meeting of
> common humanity as well as meeting the needs
> of humanity, emotional, spiritual and physical,
> with generosity. As such it mirrors the activity
> of God towards creation.[2]

I want you to foster the habit of eating with three people every week. But I want you to know that this isn't merely good missional strategy. It is a way to walk in the footsteps of Jesus.

English pastor and author Tim Chester once posed the question, "How would you complete the following sentence: 'The Son of Man came . . .'?" There are three ways that the New Testament completes that sentence; while the first two are well known (and might have come to your mind when you read Chester's question), the third is surprising:

- "The Son of Man came not to be served but to serve, and to give his life as a ransom for many" (Mark 10:45, ESV).
- "The Son of Man came to seek and to save the lost" (Luke 19:10, ESV).
- "The Son of Man came eating and drinking" (Luke 7:34).

While the first two oft-quoted verses tell us about Jesus' purpose in coming—to serve, to give his life as a ransom, to seek and save the lost—the third describes his method. How did Jesus come? He came eating and drinking.

Note that in these verses Jesus refers to himself as the "Son of Man." He uses various titles to describe himself in the Gospels, but this is one of the more dramatic. "Son of Man" comes from the apocalyptic book of Daniel and is used to describe the one who would come before God to receive authority over the nations (see Daniel 7). That Jesus attributes this apocalyptic (and somewhat esoteric) title to himself might at first sound spectacular, but he then goes on to describe this Son of Man not coming in glory on the clouds of heaven, accompanied by an army of angels, but simply eating and drinking.

It's always interested me that the one thing Jesus actually told us to do every time we meet together was to *eat*. It's not lost on me that his detractors regularly accused him of being a drunkard and a glutton (see Luke 7:34). Jesus was neither of those things, but obviously his preparedness to eat and drink with sinners, tax collectors, and prostitutes gave his enemies plenty of ammunition. So, when he comes to give his first followers something to do to remember him by, what is it? Remember Luke 22:19: "And he took bread, gave thanks and broke it, and gave it to them, saying, 'This is my body given for you; do this in remembrance of

45

me.'" Yes, the "drunkard" and the "glutton" instructed his followers to eat and drink in remembrance of him. It's beautifully subversive.

The table ought to be the primary symbol of the Christian gathering. It represents hospitality, inclusivity, generosity, and grace. In many churches today, I suppose, the primary symbol might be the pulpit or the screen. These churches seem to believe that Jesus said, "Every time you meet together, listen to a sermon and sing." Now, I'm not against sermons or singing, but if we took Jesus' directive seriously, we'd know that the table is a better metaphor for Christian worship. I love theologian (and professional chef) Simon Carey Holt's description of the table:

> It is through the daily practice of the table that we live a life worth living. Through the table we know who we are, where we come from, what we value and believe. At the table we learn what it means to be family and how to live in responsible, loving relationships. Through the table we live our neighborliness and citizenship, express our allegiance to particular places and communities, and claim our sense of home and belonging.

At the table we celebrate beauty and express solidarity with those who are broken and hungry.[3]

The invitation to share a table is a profoundly meaningful one in every culture. So I'm calling you to foster the habit of eating with three people each week. You won't need to add a great deal into your often already busy schedule. You already eat three times a day. That's twenty-one meals a week. I'm simply asking that you bring another person to your table for three of those. Or if you want to cut corners, you could bring three people to your table for one of them. Your meal could be an elaborate dinner party, or it could be breakfast, or even just coffee and a donut. Just sit across a table from three people this week, and . . . talk.

The table is the great equalizer in relationships. When we eat together we discover the inherent humanity of all people. We share stories. And hopes. And fears. And disappointments. People open up to each other. And we ourselves can open up to share the same things—including our faith in Jesus. As Alan Hirsch and Lance Ford say in their book *Right Here, Right Now*:

Sharing meals together on a regular basis is one of the most sacred practices we can engage in as believers. Missional hospitality is a tremendous opportunity to extend the kingdom of God. We can literally eat our way into the kingdom of God! If every Christian household regularly invited a stranger or a poor person into their home for a meal once a week, we would literally change the world by eating![4]

How We Shouldn't (and Should) Do It

We know that the church in Corinth was committed to holding regular love-feasts. But we also know, from Paul's correspondence with them, that they were getting it terribly wrong. Paul details his concerns here:

In the following directives I have no praise for you, for your meetings do more harm than good. In the first place, I hear that when you come together as a church, there are divisions among you, and to some extent I believe it. No doubt there have to be differences among you to show which of you have God's approval. So then, when you come together, it is not the Lord's Supper you eat, for when you are

eating, some of you go ahead with your own
private suppers. As a result, one person remains
hungry and another gets drunk. Don't you have
homes to eat and drink in? Or do you despise
the church of God by humiliating those who
have nothing?

1 CORINTHIANS 11:17-22

Paul isn't describing the kind of radical socializing that
was to turn the Roman Empire upside down. He's
describing a conflict-ridden, divisive gathering at which
the in-crowd ate, drank, and was merry while the poor
were marginalized and left hungry. And Paul is brutal
in his critique: "What shall I say to you? Shall I praise
you? Certainly not in this matter!" (verse 22).

To understand Paul's outrage, it is helpful to know
what a typical feast looked like in the Roman Empire.
Romans always maintained a ranking system at their
feasts. There was a place of honor at the head of the
dining table where the highest in rank were seated. The
host and his wife sat at the head table with the guests of
honor. The next in rank sat at the upper end, and the
third highest in social position sat at the lower end. The
meal started with the servants conducting a ceremonial

washing, moving from the highest in rank and ending with the lowest. The servants then draped the members of the dinner party with a wreath of flowers and offered them a goblet of wine. There followed a lavish meal, consisting of three to seven courses. Guests ate seated on dining couches: low seats without backs and covered with rich fabrics that could seat four people. Usually, there were three such couches. If there were more than twelve guests, the lowest-ranked took places at other tables according to social status.

Can you see how the Corinthian feast, as described by Paul, sounds very similar to any other Roman dinner party? The guests were ranked in order of importance, with certain people being left out and others appearing to eat in cliques rather than as a whole body of believers. To Paul this was contemptible. His vision was that we conduct ourselves as a radical alternative to the cruel, stratified, elitist approach of the Romans. But his answer to this problem is initially surprising:

For I received from the Lord what I also passed on to you: The Lord Jesus, on the night he was betrayed, took bread, and when he had given thanks, he broke it and said, "This is my body, which is for you; do this in remembrance of me." In the same way, after supper he took the cup, saying, "This cup is the new covenant in my blood; do this, whenever you drink it, in remembrance of me." For whenever you eat this bread and drink this cup, you proclaim the Lord's death until he comes.

So then, whoever eats the bread or drinks the cup of the Lord in an unworthy manner will be guilty of sinning against the body and blood of the Lord. Everyone ought to examine themselves before they eat of the bread and drink from the cup.

1 CORINTHIANS 11:23-28

Paul gives the Corinthians a form of words they might use in their love feasts, a kind of eucharistic liturgy that places the Lord's Supper at the center of their gathering. But how is this meant to curb their habit of elitism and party spirit? Quite brilliantly, really. Paul seems to believe that observing the habit of remembering the sacrifice of Christ every time they eat will countermand the impulse to exclude the poor or the outsider. When he insists they "examine themselves" before they eat and drink, he is asking them not to search the deepest recesses of their hearts for any unremembered and unconfessed sin (as some contemporary preachers interpret this verse) but rather to consider whom they've excluded from fellowship.

In other words, the habitual practice of the love-feast was to be an incubator in which Christians learned to accept the outsider, offer generosity to the poor, and have fellowship with those of so-called lower rank. As Paul concludes, "So then, my brothers and sisters, when you gather to eat, you should all eat *together*" (verse 33, italics added). The weekly rhythm of the communal feast was meant to help shape the Corinthians into radical socializers.

Of course, I'm not merely speaking here of inviting outsiders to your Sunday gathering. I'm suggesting our "love-feasts" should teach us how to practice hospitality throughout the week. And not only by inviting well-mannered Christian folks into our home, but also by including unbelievers or the poor at our table!

What's more, we should respond if unbelievers reciprocate our hospitality and invite us to their homes. Would our presence at their tables imply that we affirm all their values? Ben Meyer addresses this in the example of Jesus himself. After explaining that in Jesus' time a person wouldn't eat with someone of different social standing, and certainly never with someone of a different religion (for example, Jews eating at the table of Gentiles), he tells us that Jesus turned this on its head:

> The act of Jesus was to reverse this structure: communion first, conversion second. His table fellowship with sinners implied no acquiescence in their sins, for the gratuity of the reign of God cancelled none of its demands. But in a world in which sinners stood ineluctably condemned, Jesus' openness to them was irresistible. Contact triggered repentance; conversion flowered from communion. In the tense little world of ancient Palestine, where religious meanings were the warp and woof of the social order, this was a potent phenomenon.[5]

"Conversion flowered from communion." What a beautiful expression. We see it in Jesus' attendance at a meal at the home of the tax collector Zacchaeus (Luke 19:1-10). His communion with the sinful tax collector led to repentance and conversion. Likewise, we should be prepared to eat with sinners as a habitual missional practice.

I remember meeting a Southern Baptist minister in Portland who told me his neighbor both claimed to make the best margaritas in all of Oregon and regularly hosted margarita-and-poker nights in his garage. All the men from the neighborhood attended, but the Baptist pastor never accepted an invitation to join them, believing this to be a strong witness to his faith. When I heard this, I asked the pastor how many times his neighbor had asked him any questions about his faith in Christ.

"Never," he replied.

I asked how often he'd ever shared *anything* of his faith with his margarita-making neighbor; again, the answer was "Never." You see, it's not "questionable" when a Baptist refuses to attend a margarita-and-poker night. It's expected.

I challenged this pastor to accept the next invitation he received, and he took me up on it. His neighbor nearly fell over in shock. The Baptist minister joined the gathering in the garage, and true to his convictions he just drank soda. No one minded. He ended up having more conversations about faith than he'd had in ages.

The Baptist pastor at the margarita night was a surprise. It evoked questions.

All I'm asking, initially, is that you invite three people to share your table, at least one of whom isn't a churchgoer. But what you'll find happening is that people will reciprocate your hospitality. You'll start getting return invitations. And when that happens you've got serious missional traction.

Don't judge the lifestyles or eating (or drinking) habits of your host. See the opportunity as a gold mine for missional relationship building. Don't lose sight of the good goal of conversion, but follow Jesus' model of communion first and see what flowers from it.

→ *Bless three people this week—at least one of whom is not a member of your church.*

→ *Eat with three people this week—at least one of whom is not a member of your church.*

Listen: The Third Habit

I will spend at least one period of the week listening for the Spirit's voice.

The third habit I want you to foster is that of listening for the Spirit's voice. I suggest you find at least one chunk of time, preferably at the beginning of each week, to stop and create space to commune with God.

For many people, listening to the Holy Spirit is like trying to hear the radio in a busy coffee shop. You can make out the announcer's voice, but you have to strain over the hubbub of the other patrons to make out what she's saying. This is the same situation that exists when you try to listen to the Holy Spirit with too many people or things offering interference. Everything and everyone else must be "turned off."

We know the Holy Spirit is our companion and the

source of our strength, and for missionaries the Spirit is an indispensable source of wisdom. How are we to know how to negotiate our way through the world, eating with and blessing unbelievers, without the Spirit's voice to guide us away from falling into sin?

When I say "falling into sin," I don't necessarily mean getting drunk or running off with your neighbor's spouse (although of course we're never immune to making such choices). I'm referring to the much less dramatic but far more prevalent sins of fear and laziness.

Fear and laziness are mission killers. Fear of persecution, fear of standing out or causing offense, fear of having to answer someone's tricky questions—fear will shut down missional engagement every time. Likewise with laziness: I don't mean the kind of laziness that has you lying on the couch eating Doritos and watching sports on television. I mean the inner voice that prompts you not to bother with reaching out to another person, not to bother with offering yourself in the service of others. Laziness tells you that you don't have the time; laziness whispers to you that you need to take care of yourself first.

In fact, fear and laziness will motivate you to come up with dozens of reasons why you can't or shouldn't open yourself to others. It is the countermanding voice of the Spirit that will help us resist our worst impulses.

My experience when engaging with my neighbors is that I must open my heart to the Holy Spirit in order to separate truth from untruth, fiction from knowledge, the honorable from the dishonorable. Figuring out how best to be an intriguing, blessing, godly presence in community isn't easy. If I'm going to encourage you to bless others and eat with them, it would be irresponsible of me not to also encourage you to listen to the Spirit.

In his book *Satisfy Your Soul*, Bruce Demarest writes,

> A quieted heart is our best preparation for all this work of God. . . . Meditation refocuses us from ourselves and from the world so that we reflect on God's Word, His nature, His abilities, and His works. . . . So we prayerfully ponder, muse, and "chew" the words of Scripture. . . . The goal is simply to permit the Holy Spirit to activate the life-giving Word of God.[1]

When it comes to lifting or opening the heart to God the Holy Spirit, most people tend to do all of the talking and do not allow time for a reply. We have to learn how to listen. We must learn how to let the Holy Spirit do the prompting (talking). What we need to learn as missionaries is found not only in books but also in the Holy Spirit, who gives us the gift of knowledge to answer others' questions and deal with the challenges they pose.

For enthusiastic extroverts, the thought of blessing others and eating with others sounds great, but the intentional practice of solitude and silence, which is implicit in the habit of listening to the Spirit, is a big challenge. I appreciate that. Not only are extroverts disinclined to silence, but often the evangelical culture of many of our churches has been shaped by the busyness and activism of our contemporary culture, which causes us to associate mission with "doing" things. But we need to heed the warning of Dietrich Bonhoeffer: "Let him who cannot be alone beware of community. He will only do harm to himself and to the community."[2] If you find yourself being unable to be alone, it means you *need* community. And needing community can lead to you *using* community to meet your need.

Our practice of generosity and hospitality must be intentionally nurtured and sustained by the disciplines of solitude, silence, and prayer. We need to learn to listen to the voice of God, particularly as he shapes us as missionaries and fills our hearts with love for those to whom he sends us. Thomas Merton once remarked that "it is in deep solitude that I find the gentleness with which I can truly love my brothers. . . . Solitude and silence teach me to love my brothers for what they are, not for what they say."[3] Unless we can spend at least one significant period of time each week in the presence of the missional God, we are in danger of appearing no different to our frantic, harried, and busy neighbors.

This third habit will provide you with nurture, sustenance, and accountability for the missional lifestyle. Joshua and Roy Searle, from the Northumbria Community in northern England, write,

> If we regard hospitality as a missional imperative, then our participation in the *missio Dei* requires that we engage in disciplined practices, such as solitude, silence and prayer that will sustain our commitment to hospitality and lend substance and authenticity to our evangelistic and missional programs.[4]

So for those willing to undertake the challenge of silence and solitude as a missional habit, here is some advice in fostering an openness to the Spirit's promptings.

Set Aside a Designated Time

Don't try to connect to God the Holy Spirit on the run. Set aside a designated time each week. I'm only asking for one (although if you want to do it more than once a week, be my guest). See it as a precious time alone, just between you and God. Block it out in your calendar. Let people know that Monday night or Saturday morning, or whatever time you designate, is your time of solitude.

Eliminate Distractions

For the person untrained in listening to the Holy Spirit, you should find ways to avoid any intrusion on the senses of touch, sight, smell, taste, or sound. Music, noise in the distance, the tick of a clock, voices of people, the gentle breeze of the wind, even the written words of others in inspirational books—each can prove to be a distraction and prompt us to listen to what our ears or other senses are picking up. The quieter the room or surroundings, the more conducive to listening to the Holy Spirit. After all, Jesus taught us, "When you pray, go into your room, close the door and pray . . . in secret" (Matthew 6:6).

Find a comfortable position in a chair and adopt the posture most helpful to you for spiritual concentration. Lacing your fingers together, placing your palms together, or sitting on your hands can help you become less conscious of them. Closing your eyes in a dark or semidark room can help to eliminate any visual distractions. If at all possible, be prepared to sit for twenty minutes or more. Something often happens to the stillness around ten to fifteen minutes in; if you stop too soon, you will miss it.

After eliminating all of these distractions, you will be ready to listen.

Let God In

Don't start your meditation by asking questions or telling the Holy Spirit what you want. He already knows. Start by simply enjoying God's presence. Sit quietly and let the Holy Spirit possess you. The devil most likely will try to discourage you, reminding you of your sins and unworthiness. You must always remember that God loves you because he created you. While you may be well aware of your unworthiness, the Holy Spirit is most anxious to dwell in your heart, the temple he created for himself. In times like this I am conscious of the words of St. Thérèse of Lisieux: "If you are willing to bear serenely the trial of being displeasing to yourself, then you will be for Jesus a pleasant place of shelter."[5]

If you're an outcomes-oriented person, you'll be desperate to get to the point of it and ask the Spirit to grant you knowledge or wisdom or courage or righteousness, or whatever you need in your current circumstance. But before you get to that, simply abide in his presence. Let his love wash over you.

Use what's called a centering prayer to focus your attention. Some people use the ancient Christian prayer-word *maranatha* ("Our Lord has come"). Others use the so-called Jesus Prayer, adapted from Luke 18:13: "Lord Jesus Christ, Son of God, have mercy on me, a sinner." Other common centering prayers are words such as *amen, Abba, grace, love, peace, let go, stillness, Jesus.* Choose one if it helps, but note: It isn't a mantra. You don't need to chant it. It's a prayer, and by repeating it slowly and gently you help to center yourself on hearing God. Praying in this way helps you to bring all those random thoughts, and all your normal edginess, under control. As Thomas Merton said, "The prayer of the heart has to be always very simple, confined to the simplest of acts."[6]

Remember that centering prayer is different from classic Eastern meditation, which is attempting to empty your mind by pushing thoughts away or by having no thoughts. Christian contemplative practices expert Phil Fox Rose says that when engaging in centering prayer, the key is to "resist no thought; retain no thought; react to no thought."[7] Most of us simply can't stop thinking anyway. Our minds are constantly racing. If we make having no thoughts the goal, we'll get discouraged. Rose continues, "In centering prayer, we let thoughts happen, but we don't engage them." After a period of time of centering prayer, you'll find your thoughts slowing down, becoming more captive to the object of your worship, more shaped by the Holy Spirit. After time you'll learn to read which thoughts are God's thoughts.

Listening to the Holy Spirit can become for you, just as it has for me, a source of comfort, a source of great peace, a source of answers to present problems. Listening to God can be one of the highest forms of prayer.

Follow God's Promptings

The Spirit might bring to your mind the name or the face of a person you are to bless or eat with (which is why you might want to begin your week with this exercise). The Spirit might convict you of sin or encourage you in your faithfulness. The Spirit might prompt you to reengage with someone you blessed last week, or he might bring to mind something you ought to have said to someone but didn't. You will sense his presence in your heart, that presence will add strength to your arm and oxygen to your soul, and you will be filled with his rewards: love, joy, peace, or any of the other fruit of the Holy Spirit.

In Romans 8, Paul presents the stark difference between those who "live according to . . . what the flesh desires" and those who "have their minds set on what the Spirit desires" (v. 5). While some people have mistakenly interpreted this in an overly dualistic way (flesh is bad; spirit is good), I understand Paul to be talking about the worldview that the believer adopts. If we are governed entirely by our appetites, we will be driven in very unhelpful directions. If, however, we allow the Spirit to guide us, we will be free to enjoy our appetites in a redeemed, godly fashion.

All that to say, missionaries *really* need to know how to rein in their appetites by setting their minds on what the Spirit desires. If I go back to what I said earlier about eating and drinking with unbelievers (an essential missionary practice), we need to be governed by the Spirit's promptings to ensure we are a godly example, one that arouses curiosity and interest in our faith. Carousing and gossiping like anyone else isn't all that interesting to anyone. Eating and drinking and blessing others in the way of the Spirit will be surprising to others.

The difficulty for many people seeking to live missional lives is negotiating the spectrum between being withdrawn and judgmental on the one hand and entering fully into a social setting that might be considered ungodly on the other.

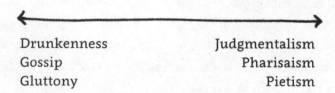

Drunkenness	Judgmentalism
Gossip	Pharisaism
Gluttony	Pietism

The extremes of missional presence: engagement versus withdrawal

Truly missional Christians aren't happy to be at either end of the spectrum. And yet the "rules" associated with either end of the spectrum are much easier to figure out. We get what total withdrawal from social settings with unbelievers looks like. We know what it's like to spend all our social time with fellow believers. Likewise, it's easy to simply go with the flow and fit in socially with our neighbors and look no different to them. Total withdrawal and total capitulation both make sense. It's far trickier to work out the balance or the tension between withdrawal and engagement.

Trying to figure out how to sit somewhere in the middle—a godly, intriguing, socially adventurous, joyous presence in the lives of others—is tough. I don't think we're clever enough on our own to find that balance. That's where the missional voice of the Spirit comes in. His promptings help us adjust our stance. The Spirit's promptings rebuke us when we drift too far to either end of the spectrum, choreographing our social lives in a way that promotes connection with unbelievers while also rousing their curiosity about our faith. And as we become more familiar with listening to the Spirit as a kind of weekly rhythm, we'll also find ourselves becoming more adept at hearing the Spirit in real time, in the midst of encounters with our neighbors, as we bless or share a meal or otherwise get in the way of the people around us. That's why listening to the Spirit is one of the five habits of highly missional people.

→ *Bless three people this week—at least one of whom is not a member of your church.*

→ *Eat with three people this week—at least one of whom is not a member of your church.*

→ *Spend at least one period of the week listening for the Spirit's voice.*

Learn: The Fourth Habit

I will spend at least one period
of the week learning Christ.

The expression "to learn Christ" was a common one among the earliest Christians, but it's not a phrase we use much these days. In the early centuries of the Christian movement, conversion involved denying the pagan gods and entering a period of catechism, committing oneself to an intensive study of the person and work of Jesus. We would do well to institute a habitual study of the Gospels ourselves today.

There are two primary reasons why I'm commending this emphasis on learning Jesus. One is the devotional value of growing closer to Jesus, fostering intimacy with God, hearing the promptings of the Spirit, and sensing his presence though the beauty of his Word in your life. There is also great devotional value in learning Jesus' teaching and seeking to conform your life more and more to his will. But there's a second, more missional reason why I want you to learn Jesus. We need to know him if we're going to share him as the reason for the hope we have.

In fact, when we're living questionable lives, both the devotional and missional purposes for studying the Gospels intersect. I think that if we're being sent into the world to live intriguing lives, arouse curiosity, and answer people's inquiries about the hope we have within, we need more than ever to know what Jesus would do or say in any circumstance. And we can't know that without a deep and ongoing study of the biographies of Jesus written by those who knew him best—the Gospels.

Some years ago, Alan Hirsch and I wrote a book about this. It was our contention in *ReJesus* that the church needs to be immersed again in the Gospels, totally marinated in the work and words of Jesus. In making this argument we were taking our lead from C. S. Lewis, who wrote:

> In the same way the Church exists for nothing else but to draw [people] into Christ, to make them little Christs. If they are not doing that, all the cathedrals, clergy, missions, sermons, even the

Bible itself, are simply a waste of time. God became Man for no other purpose. It is even doubtful, you know, whether the whole universe was created for any other purpose. It says in the Bible that the whole universe was made for Christ and that everything is to be gathered together in Him.[1]

Some readers will be disturbed by Lewis's reference to us becoming "little Christs," but he isn't proposing anything blasphemous here. Rather, he is promoting a preoccupation with the example and teaching of Jesus for the purposes of emulation by his followers. Of course, we can't emulate Christ in his salvific death and resurrection, his miracles, and his judgment of the unrighteous. But we *can* embrace a study and examination of the person and work of Jesus, helping us to determine how the various elements of his character and activity can be emulated by us as sinful human beings. For example, we *can't* die for others like Jesus did, but we *can* offer ourselves sacrificially in service of others. "Learning Christ" helps us understand Jesus better and provides the tools for appropriating his example into our lives.

I'm not saying that we should simply mine the Gospels for life advice on how to answer the question

"What would Jesus do?" We need to be students of the whole of Scripture, which includes understanding the Gospels in their total biblical context. I agree with theologian John Stackhouse when he says,

> "What did Jesus say?" . . . is the wrong question for Christian thought just as "What would Jesus do?" is the wrong question for Christian ethics. "What would Jesus want me or us to think, be, and do, here and now?" is the right question.[2]

My concern is that many Christians seem to have developed merely a passing knowledge of the Gospels (what I call Jesus' greatest hits—his birth, his death, his resurrection, a few miracles, and a couple of parables). If we are to figure out what Jesus would want us to think, be, and do here and now, we must know the Gospels forward and backward.

Is This What You Call "Incarnational" Mission?

You might have heard people referring to the church's need to embrace an *incarnational* stance in mission. You may have wondered exactly what that means. The term *mission* (from the Latin *missio*) means "to be sent; to be propelled outward." Lots of churches seem to get the idea that to be *missional* we must go out to others with the Good News, rather than merely wait for people to come to us. But the term *incarnational* refers to another dimension of mission. It describes not simply going out but also the difficult work of going deep with others. Just as God took on flesh and dwelt among us in Jesus, so his followers are called to *dwell among* those to whom they're sent. Missiologist Ross Langmead describes it this way:

> Mission can be labeled incarnational in the sense of (1) being patterned on the Incarnation, (2) being enabled by the continuing power of the Incarnation, and (3) joining the ongoing incarnating mission of God.[3]

So if I'm calling people to live an incarnational life, I'm asking them to pattern their lives on the Incarnation (with a capital *I*). How are we to do that—unless we become avid students of the life, work, and teaching of Jesus? How are we to truly dwell among the neighbors to whom God has sent us—patterning ourselves on the example of Jesus, figuring out what Jesus would do in any instance ("Would Jesus attend that Super Bowl party on a Sunday? Would he laugh at that colleague's joke? Would he disagree with that neighbor's opinion?")—without fostering the habit of learning the Gospels?

Spending just one chunk of time on learning Christ is no great sacrifice. But I hasten to point out that you should also continue with whatever other regular Bible reading habit you currently have. It would be wrong for me to imply that the Gospels are the *only* biblical material you need to study. John Stackhouse warns against preferencing the Gospels to the exclusion of the rest of the Bible. He gives four reasons why we should, yes, study the Gospels, but *in the context of* studying the rest of Scripture. I paraphrase them this way:

1. Even though the Gospels appear first in our New Testament, they are not the earliest written documents about Jesus. Paul's early letters predate the four Gospels; if we're only interested in the earliest record, Paul's writings would earn a higher priority.
2. We shouldn't be privileging only what we assume to be the oldest material, since all Scripture is the Word of God.

3. Privileging the Gospels might make sense if we believed the Gospels were written by Jesus himself, but of course they weren't.
4. Jesus, as part of the Triune Godhead, is the author of the whole Bible, not just the Gospels.[4]

Stackhouse concludes with this majestic statement:

> While the story of Jesus is indeed the key to history, to emphasize the Gospels over the rest of the New Testament is to forget that Jesus is Lord over *all* of history, Jesus is Head of the church that succeeds him in earthly ministry, and Jesus is in fact the Author of the *whole* New Testament via the inspiration of the Holy Spirit—as he is, indeed, the God who inspired the whole Bible.[5]

I agree. So, when I tell you to spend at least one significant period of time studying the Gospels each week, I'm asking you not to do that in isolation from your broader biblical study. I expect that your church hosts regular Bible study groups with a predetermined curriculum.

Stick with that. You might use a personal study guide with daily readings from across the whole Bible. Stick with that, too. I'm asking you to add a meaningful study of the earliest biographies of Jesus so you are better able to answer the questions people raise about him and learn more and more how to pattern your life on the Incarnation.

Let me suggest three things you might do with your time.

1. *Study the Gospels.* Read, reread, and reread again the four canonical Gospels. I know you think you've done that before, but I'm asking you to develop a habit of really marinating your mind and your soul in the four Gospels.

You might want to mix up the manner of your reading. Consider taking the time to read one or another of them through in one sitting. Mark will take about ninety minutes, John about two hours, and you can get through Matthew and Luke in around two and a half hours each. Reading them in one sitting helps you to connect to their broad themes and the rhythms of their language.

Of course, you can also read the Gospels in sections. And you can read them with the use of commentaries or daily devotional material. All I'm asking is that you cultivate a habit of constantly reconnecting with Jesus through the words of Scripture.

2. Read about Jesus. There are so many scholarly and popular works written about Jesus that it might be hard to choose. I have written a couple: *Jesus the Fool* (Baker, 2010) looks at the way Jesus reframes our conventional wisdom;[6] *ReJesus*, my book with Alan Hirsch about the need for the church to rediscover Jesus and his message, is useful for church leaders.[7] I would also strongly recommend scholarly works like *The Challenge of Jesus* by N. T. Wright, *Jesus According to Scripture* by Darrell Bock, *Jesus and the Gospels* by Craig Blomberg, and anything about Jesus by Ben Witherington. At a more popular level, check out Tim Keller's *King's Cross*.[8] (I've included a list of more great books as an appendix.)

Your church might consider developing a collection of reading material—including chapters from preferred books, articles, and blogs—to help reinforce the learning of Christ throughout the congregation.

3. Further viewing. Why not develop a library of filmed versions of the Gospels? Since no one single depiction of Jesus' life on film can adequately do him justice, I find it helpful to explore a range of films to get a better sense of what the Gospels teach. A couple of them—*Godspell* and *Jesus of Montreal*—aren't technically films about Jesus himself, but they beautifully capture different aspects of Jesus' character and action. And don't forget the charming 2000 animated film *The Miracle Maker*, in which the day-to-day experiences of Jesus are depicted with stop-motion puppets, while the parables, flashbacks, memories, and spiritual encounters are depicted the traditional, hand-drawn way. Very clever. I have listed some of my other favorites in the appendix. And if you don't like some of the grittier films in my list, there are plenty more available, all freely searchable online.

You might have picked up earlier on my reference to us needing to *marinate* our minds and souls in the story of Jesus. It's not just a cute expression. I meant it. Through biblical study, theological reading, and even the viewing of films (no matter how limited each of them might be), we slowly but surely orient our lives toward the things of Christ, and we become deeply familiar with his story so we can share it whenever anyone asks us for the reason for the hope we have in him.

The Way Surfers Talk about Kelly Slater

One of the beautiful things that happens to people who marinate their minds in the Gospels is that they start to talk about Jesus like he's their hero, their friend, their king. Some years ago, I was speaking at a conference for a parachurch ministry called Christian Surfers in Australia. Christian Surfers is an awesome ministry that aims to share Jesus with young surfers. They have chapters based in beachside towns and suburbs all around the world. This conference was for their staff workers from around Australia. During one of my sessions I asked the attendees—all hardcore surfing enthusiasts—to name their favorite surfer of all time. Now, when you ask a room full of keen surfers to name their surfing hero, the room erupts. I heard a number of different names being called out, but the name I heard the most was that of Florida surfer Kelly Slater.

I wasn't surprised. Slater has been crowned the world surfing champion a record eleven times, including five consecutive times from 1994 to 1998. He is both the youngest (at age twenty) and the oldest (at age thirty-nine) to win the title.

"Okay, okay," I called out to the excitable audience.

"Let's choose Kelly Slater as our example. So, what do you all know about Kelly Slater?"

This time the room didn't just erupt, it combusted. When I asked a bunch of surfers to tell me what they knew about undoubtedly the most successful surfer in all of history, they went nuts! They were yelling and screaming facts about Slater's life—where he grew up (Cocoa Beach), what boards he uses (Channel Island surfboards), which years he won the title (too many to list here), what movies and television shows he's appeared in (too many to list here), which models and movie stars he's dated (again, too many to list here), and on and on. It was pandemonium. And it took a while to quiet them all down again.

Later in the session I was talking about our need to marinate our minds in the Gospels so we can share Jesus as the reason for the hope we have, so I asked them, "Tell me, what do you all know about Jesus?" The response this time was very different. It wasn't as if these folks didn't know anything about Jesus. They're highly committed evangelists. In fact, they lead many young surfers to Christ every year. But the response was much more muted. Slowly, quietly, people offered things they knew about Jesus ("He's Lord," "He died for our sins," "He rose from the dead"), but these were presented as doctrinal beliefs, statements of faith. I asked them why they didn't speak about Jesus in the same way that they had just been telling me about Kelly Slater. Again, crickets.

It seems to me that this is our challenge today. As I mentioned earlier, I don't think every Christian is an evangelist, but I do think every Christian should be evangelistic. When we live questionable lives, people should see our strange behavior and ask us about our motivations. And when they do, we should be able to speak about Jesus the way surfers speak about Kelly Slater: with energy and enthusiasm, with reverence and awe, with delight and wonder.

→ *Bless three people this week—at least one of whom is not a member of your church.*

→ *Eat with three people this week—at least one of whom is not a member of your church.*

→ *Spend at least one period of the week listening for the Spirit's voice.*

→ *Spend at least one period of the week learning Christ.*

Sent: The Fifth Habit

I will journal throughout the week all
the ways I alerted others to the universal reign
of God through Christ.

*The final habit is to begin identifying yourself as a
missionary—a sent one—*by journaling the ways you're
alerting others to God's reign. You can make daily journal entries or set aside some time at the end of each
week to look back over the last seven days to recall how
you've either announced or demonstrated God's universal reign, even if it's in the smallest of ways.

Earlier I mentioned that our English term *mission*
comes from the Latin *missio*, which means to send
or to be ejected or pushed out. The word was almost
exclusively used to describe a person who travels over-
seas attempting to spread Christianity. More recently,
we've adopted the term to describe all Christians who

attempt to glorify God in their daily lives. If our mission is to alert others to the universal reign of God through Christ, then all believers should see themselves as missionaries.

Again, this doesn't mean every believer is a gifted evangelist. But it does mean that every believer needs to take seriously his or her calling to alert others to God's reign and rule. In my book *The Road to Missional*, I refer to our lives being like a trailer or a preview for an upcoming feature film:

> Trailers are tasters, short film versions of the soon-to-released feature, and they usually include the best special effects or the funniest scenes or the most romantic moments, depending on the film, of the upcoming feature. Now, watch those around you in the theatre at the end of each trailer. If it has done its job, usually one person will turn to the other and say, "I want to see that movie."
>
> This is a great metaphor for the missional church. If it does its job well, people will see what it does and say, "I want to see the world they come from."[1]

Some questions necessarily follow: Well then, what does the reign of God look like? If your life is meant to alert people to his reign, what exactly are you pointing them toward?

Let me suggest a few things. I have borrowed them from various writings by N. T. Wright and have explained them in greater detail in *The Road to Missional*.[2]

Reconciliation

Since reconciliation between God and humankind is at the heart of Christ's work on the cross, it makes sense that reconciliation—between God and human-kind, between Jew and Gentile, slave and free, black and white and Asian and Hispanic, and so on—should be a core expression of God's reign and rule. We are to both announce reconciliation (champion it, describe it, explain it, advocate for it), and demonstrate it (be reconciled to others, broker reconciliation among others).

For this fifth missional habit, I want you to start journaling all the ways in any given week you've alerted others (by word or by deed) to the *reconciling* aspect of God's reign. You might have done this in your work-place by mediating between warring colleagues. Or you might have reconciled with a friend or relative from whom you've been estranged. You might have shared the Good News with someone that God reconciles us to himself through his Son, Jesus. The more you journal this stuff, the more you find yourself living it out.

Justice

It's not true to say, as many do, that evangelicals have only just begun to be interested in social justice. In fact, Christians have long recognized in Scripture a call to defend and uphold the dignity and well-being of all persons, especially the poor and powerless. They have seen this as a primary expression of the reign of God, a kingdom in which everyone has enough and no one is marginalized or disadvantaged. Christian greats such as John Wesley, Lord Shaftesbury, Charles Spurgeon, and Charles Finney led campaigns for the betterment of society, whether it was prison reform, labor reform, the abolition of slavery, or the temperance movement. More recently, Christian leaders like Mother Teresa, Martin Luther King, Desmond Tutu, Dorothy Day, John Stott, and Jim Wallis have promoted Christian engagement in antipoverty, antiwar, environmental, and immigration causes.

Today there are all kinds of ways we can be sent to demonstrate this aspect of God's reign, whether it be eliminating sex trafficking, promoting fair-trade products, campaigning for clean water, or some other specific cause. There are now new movements to encourage Christians to fight homelessness and to foster disadvantaged children. Whether you're simply donating to a cause, signing an online petition, or opening your home to the poor, start journaling the ways you were sent to show justice in your world this week.

Beauty

When I mention "beauty" as a missional priority, people are sometimes surprised. Reconciliation and justice make sense. The Bible is full of references to such things. But beauty as an expression of the reign of God? Really? But the more you think about it, the more sense it makes. Where else do you often feel closest to God but on a mountaintop or at a beach or in the presence of natural beauty? Doesn't a beautiful cathedral or a piece of music leverage you toward the Creator of all true beauty?

Some years ago I was moved to tears listening to some music (it was just music, not "Christian music"), and I remember wondering why music existed. The only conclusion I could come to was that it is a gift of God to his people, Christian and non-Christian alike, and that we could see God in it even if it was written by a lascivious Mozart rather than a godly Wesley. C. S. Lewis suspected as much when he wrote:

> For the beasts can't appreciate it [beauty] and
> the angels are, I suppose, pure intelligences.
> They *understand* colors and tastes better than
> our greatest scientists; but have they retinas or
> palates? I fancy the "beauties of nature" are a
> secret God has shared with us alone. That may
> be one of the reasons why we were made.[3]

If beauty is an expression of God's reign, we need to think about ways to invite our friends to encounter it. Take them hiking. Climb mountains. Walk along beaches. Encounters with true beauty can't help but make us think of Psalm 8: "When I consider . . . the work of your fingers, . . . what is mankind that you are mindful of them?"

Rudolph Otto, a German theologian, listed a number

of responses normally associated with an awe-encounter with God. They include a sense of majesty, unapproachability, and a feeling of fascination, including both fear and attraction. He also speaks of a feeling that can never be adequately described, only experienced—the feeling that we are important enough to be invited to encounter the Holy (as Otto called it), but in its presence we are overwhelmed and made aware of our smallness. Such experiences of the transcendent are not only frightening; they are also strangely comforting. We need them.

But more than just enjoying natural beauty, I think we should commit ourselves both to creating beautiful music, art, craft, and food and to inviting others to join us. Try to find ways to alert others to the universal reign of God through Christ by an observation of his creation and by personally fashioning expressions of beauty. And when you do, make a record of it in your journal.

Wholeness

In Luke 7, the imprisoned John the Baptist sends his followers to double-check that Jesus really is the Messiah. Jesus' response to their questioning of his identity is really interesting:

> Go back and report to John what you have seen
> and heard: The blind receive sight, the lame
> walk, those who have leprosy are cleansed, the
> deaf hear, the dead are raised, and the good
> news is proclaimed to the poor.
>
> LUKE 7:22

In other words, the "credentials" Jesus presented to prove
he was the Messiah, ushering in the universal reign of
God, were the restoration of broken people. Jesus healed
the blind, the lame, the lepers, and the deaf—and even
raised the dead—as evidence of God's kingdom coming
in glory. Therefore, it should be reasonable to suggest
that *wholeness*, the healing of broken people, is primary
evidence of that reign today.

Of course, many Christians—doctors, nurses, psy-
chologists, and counselors, for example—are committed to bringing healing to the lives of others. And I want
to encourage these as important expressions of the reign
of God. When Christians provide emergency relief to
victims of natural disasters, we are showing what the
reign of God looks like. When we help to repair a broken marriage, we do the same. When a Christian medi-
cal practitioner treats patients with dignity and grace,

bringing healing to their bodies, we can clearly see it as mirroring the work of God. But I want to go further and say that, more than these practical expressions of healing, we should also be praying for *supernatural* healing in people's lives. And when we observe supernatural healing, we should keep a record of it in our journals, a reminder to ourselves that our healing work is merely a mirror of the work of the Great Physician.

But Why Journaling?

Why do I want you to journal your experience? Well, as Anne Broyles says, in keeping a journal, "what our mind is thinking and our heart is feeling becomes tangible: ink on paper."[4] Indeed, journaling is more than just a way of thinking things through: It is a recognized spiritual discipline. More than just recording your thoughts, however, I want you to identify ways you mirrored God's work of justice, reconciliation, beauty, and wholeness in the world. This will be more than writing, "I shared Christ with someone today" or "I treated a confused student kindly today." It will be about helping you to sort through the myriad everyday ways you operate as God's ambassador in your world. I want you to explore how your commitments to craftsmanship, care, and commerce reflect the things of the kingdom.

Journaling has plenty of benefits in itself, but this kind of habitual, missional journaling will be helpful in the following ways.

Processing events. What you've done during the previous week is only as important as the meaning you assign to it. Without stopping to process your actions, you might not see that healing your patients, teaching your students, raising your children, or producing nutritious food or beautiful art or excellent workmanship are ways you mirror God's work in the world. Journaling helps you sort through your experiences and be intentional about your interpretation of them. It helps you to see everyday acts—of creativity, diligence, service, and kindness—as being as legitimately missional as acts of evangelism, preaching, or social justice.

Making sense of God's work. You're busy, I know. Life is happening so quickly, and most people don't take the time to stop and truly reflect on what really means the most to us. We get the job done. We complete our required tasks. We put the kids to bed. We try to keep fit. But when do you stop to ask where God is in the midst of your work, your family, your leisure time?

Journaling forces you to take notice of the way God is unfurling his reign throughout the world through your small contributions on earth.

Keeping a record of insights. We're all better students when we're taking notes. Writing things down leads to an even deeper understanding of the ways God is using you and a clearer vision of what his reign looks like in your world. Write down what you're learning, and you can read back through earlier entries and see the pattern of discovery that's been unfolding in your life.

Asking important questions. You'll be surprised how much of your journaling takes the form of questions. You'll find yourself writing, "Was that you, God?" or "I loved repairing so-and-so's car today, but is that really an expression of God's work in the world?" or "When I said such-and-such to my colleague, was that you speaking through me, Jesus?" The more we journal, the better our questions become. And the better our questions become, the better the answers will be.

Feel free to express your feelings, your doubts, and your uncertainties. Feelings aren't everything, but they also aren't nothing. Try to pay attention to them. They are often an early indicator of the condition of your heart. Journaling helps you to get off autopilot and to genuinely focus on what you're feeling about your missional presence in your workplace or your neighborhood, and to ask questions about God, his reign, and your place in it.

Identifying ourselves differently. People wear fitness-monitoring wristbands that record the number of steps they walk, their sleep patterns, and their calorie intake. Then they sync those stats wirelessly to their phones or computers and track their overall progress. When you think about it, this is a form of journaling. It's a way of recording your development. It defines you in some meaningful way as a person concerned about your physical fitness.

Keeping a journal and recording all the ways you are mirroring God's work in the world is similar. It will start to shape the way you think about yourself. You will eventually come to self-identify as a missionary, a *sent one*. You'll be looking at your life and how you conduct yourself differently, and the journaling process will reinforce this in creative and useful ways.

This is the key to this fifth habit. It is about reshaping our identities around our fundamental calling as the sent ones of God. By fostering the habit of briefly journaling the various ways (large or small) in which you alerted others to God's reign of reconciliation, justice, beauty, and wholeness, you will find yourself increasingly identifying yourself as a sent one. And remember that you can alert others to these things both by talking about them (witness) and by demonstrating them (action).

→ *Bless three people this week—at least one of whom is not a member of your church.*

→ *Eat with three people this week—at least one of whom is not a member of your church.*

→ *Spend at least one period of the week listening for the Spirit's voice.*

→ *Spend at least one period of the week learning Christ.*

→ *Journal throughout the week all the ways you alerted others to the universal reign of God through Christ.*

(8)

Discipleship, Nurture, and Accountability

As should be obvious by now, I'm not merely promoting these five practices as a one-off program. I want you to make a habit of them. I want you to inculcate these habits as a central rhythm of your life. You see, doing a short-term project, like *Forty Days of Purpose*, is great.[1] But missional effectiveness grows exponentially the longer we embrace these habits and the deeper we go with them.

How long does it take for us to form a habit? In his book *Making Habits, Breaking Habits: Why We Do Things, Why We Don't, and How to Make Any Change Stick*, Jeremy Dean suggests that it takes much longer than we have assumed. Dean's research involved asking a hundred participants to choose an everyday behavior that they wanted to turn into a habit. They all chose something they didn't already do that could be repeated every day. Many were health-related: People chose things like "eating a piece of fruit with lunch" and "running for fifteen minutes after dinner." For eighty-four days they logged into a website and reported whether or not they'd carried out the behavior, as well as how automatic the behavior had felt. Dean found the following:

> The simple answer is that, on average, across the participants who provided enough data, it took 66 days until a habit was formed. As you might imagine, there was considerable variation in how long habits took to form depending on what people tried to do. People who resolved to drink a glass of water after breakfast were up to maximum automaticity after about 20 days, while those trying to eat a piece of fruit with lunch took at least twice as long to turn it into a habit. The exercise habit proved most tricky with "50 sit-ups after morning coffee," still not a habit after 84 days for one participant. "Walking for 10 minutes after breakfast,"

though, was turned into a habit after 50 days for another participant.[2]

From Dean's research it seems that it might only take a few weeks to develop a basic habit like drinking a glass of water every day, but to change and develop new habits that are more complex can take months of intentional practice. Now, I'm asking you to do something considerably more challenging than eating a piece of fruit with lunch. For that reason, I propose that a simple system of accountability needs to be put in place to ensure that you remain committed to these habits over a long period of time.

My suggestion is that you build a triad of accountability, a microgroup of three people that meets weekly to hold each member accountable to the habits, as well as encouraging and nurturing each other and helping each other learn from their experience of living out the habits. I call these microgroups DNAs (Discipleship, Nurture, Accountability). You might be familiar with Neil Cole's Life Transformation Groups, which have a similar format.[3]

DNA groups meet weekly to ask and answer a series of accountability questions. I propose that the questions be shaped around the five habits, and at the end of this chapter I have included a suggested accountability form that each member might complete in preparation for each meeting. It includes such questions as "Whom have I blessed this week?" and "What did I hear from the Holy Spirit this week?" It also includes more open-ended questions, such as "What questions, issues, or learning arose from this habit this week?"

My hope for DNA meetings is that each member might not only report on whether they completed the habits that week but also begin to allow themselves to be shaped as missionaries by those habits. A DNA meeting should fulfill the following goals.

Discipleship. By asking each other about what questions, issues, or learning were stimulated by the five habits, the members of your DNA group can help you process your responses and move forward with greater insight and confidence. For example, if you ate with someone who confessed he or she had marriage problems, your fellow members might help you explore recommended strategies for him or her. If a neighbor stumped you by raising questions about same-sex marriage, told you they were exploring Buddhism, or asked questions about an area of the Bible you weren't familiar with, your DNA friends could help you think through ways you might have responded more appropriately. Together you could study the Scriptures to develop biblical responses to those issues.

Furthermore, by sharing with each other what you've learned about Jesus that week, you will be teaching each other from the Word of God. In other words, you'll be discipling each other based on your missional experiences through the five habits.

Nurture. If you've had an unusually busy week, your kids are sick or won't sleep, or you're feeling depleted and unable to give any more, you can share this with your DNA group. The DNA process isn't designed to beat you up when you fall short and can't fulfill the five habits. It's there to encourage you and support you when things get overwhelming.

Accountability. Having said that, if you didn't fulfill the five habits this week because of laziness or fear, your DNA group is there to provide some real accountability. They are to hold you to the commitments you made together. Knowing that your friends are checking in on you should provide some impetus to continue with the habits.

Moreover, if the Spirit convicted you of the need

for repentance in an area of your life, you might confess this in your DNA group so that they can hold you accountable to whatever new choices the Spirit's voice has called you to. If the teachings of Jesus have prompted you to set different priorities, you can share this with your DNA group and ask them to hold you accountable to it.

As we discovered earlier, to make these five commitments (blessing, eating, listening, learning, sentness) a set of habits, we need to stick with them for an extended period of time. The discipleship, nurturing, and accountability built into DNA groups are essential to help you stay at it. But remember, I'm not asking you to do something distasteful or unpleasant. Blessing people is personally satisfying. Eating with others is fun. Listening to the Spirit and learning about Jesus is spiritually enriching. And journaling the various ways you alert others to the reign of God is encouraging.

→ *Who in your life would make for a good DNA relationship? Read this book with those people, and commit together to regular touchpoints for mutual discernment, nurturing, and accountability.*

THE BELLS CHALLENGE
DNA Accountability Form

BLESS: Whom Did I Bless This Week?

_____ _____ _____ _____

_____ _____ _____ _____

_____ _____ _____ _____

What questions, issues, or learning arose
from this habit this week?

_____

_____

_____

EAT: With Whom Did I Eat This Week?

_____ _____ _____ _____

_____ _____ _____ _____

_____ _____ _____ _____

(continued on next page)

What questions, issues, or learning arose
from this habit this week?

_____

_____

_____

LISTEN: What Did I Hear from
the Holy Spirit This Week?

_____

_____

_____

LEARN: What Did I Learn (or Relearn)
about Christ This Week?

_____

_____

_____

SENT: Share Two or Three Journal Entries about How You Alerted Others to the Reign of God

_____

_____

_____

_____

_____

_____

_____

_____

_____

QUESTIONS FOR DISCUSSION AND ENGAGEMENT

Use any or all of the following questions to stimulate conversation and the practice of the five habits among your friends and fellow believers.

A SURPRISING FAITH (CHAPTERS 1–2)

1. The author sees engaging neighbors, connecting with each other, experiencing God's leading, understanding Jesus' life and teaching, and understanding ourselves as missionaries each as "essential" aspects of Christian faith. What do you think makes them essential?

2. Which of those "essentials" are most natural or comfortable for you? Which of them are difficult for you?

3. Are we really all evangelists? Do you know anyone who is a gifted evangelist in the manner the author describes?

4. Do you feel pressure as a Christian to "act like evangelists"? In what ways do you most typically "share" your faith with or "demonstrate" it to your friends and neighbors?

5. Does the twofold approach to evangelism described by the author ring true for you? Why or why not?

6. Have you ever heard the description of the "surprising" behavior of the early church and its impact on Roman culture? What surprises you about it?

7. In what ways do you see the contemporary church surprising (or failing to surprise) the broader culture through its behavior?

8. The author suggests that Christian philanthropy and "a fine, upstanding middle-class lifestyle" are not "questionable" in a way that leads people to faith. Why do you think that is? What makes a behavior "questionable" or "surprising"?

A RELATIONAL FAITH (CHAPTERS 3–4)

1. "Faith, then, is not an act, a single choice, or even just a belief system; it is a *habit*." Does this ring true for you? What is the difference between faith as a habit and faith as any of these other things?

2. "Behavior change involves the challenge of familiarization." What aspects of your faith life have become overfamiliar? In what ways might the church have become overfamiliar to the broader culture?

3. Who in your life has "added strength to your arm"? How have their acts of blessing informed your faith?

4. Which of the types of blessing—words of affirmation, acts of kindness, gift giving—is most natural and comfortable for you? Which did you find yourself engaging in as you developed a habit of blessing through this book?

5. How can you become a better "student" of the people you bless?

6. How do you sustain your commitment to bless when people misunderstand your motives or mock your faith?

7. "Eating with others can be perceived as a profoundly *theological* practice." Does this ring true to you? As you think about meals you've shared with others, what do they show and tell you about God?

8. "The table is the great equalizer in relationships." How so? How have shared meals enriched your relationships?

9. How has taking on the habits of blessing others and of eating together shaped your faith lately? In what ways have these habits surprised your friends and neighbors?

A RECEPTIVE FAITH (CHAPTERS 5–6)

1. Reflect on your history of prayer and contemplation. When have you found it hard to hear the Spirit's voice speaking into your life? When have you found yourself particularly open to the Spirit's voice? What has made the difference?

2. Do you find solitude, silence, and prayer to be enriching or intimidating? Both? Neither? What about these habits appeals to you?

3. What challenges do you face in setting aside time to listen for the Spirit's voice? What would help you protect that time as a regular habit?

4. Where do you find yourself on the spectrum between missional engagement and withdrawal? How do you want the Spirit to support you in finding the right missional posture?

5. What do you see as the difference between reading (or studying) the Bible and "learning Christ"?

6. What do you find surprising, questionable, and intriguing about Jesus, based on what you've already learned about him?

7. What does it mean for us to pattern our lives on the Incarnation of Jesus? Where do you see the Incarnation informing your daily life?

8. Can you imagine yourself being as excitable about Jesus as surfers are about Kelly Slater? What gets in the way of that excitement for you?

9. How has taking on the habits of listening for the Spirit and learning Christ shaped your faith lately? In what ways have these habits surprised your friends and neighbors?

A SHARED FAITH (CHAPTERS 7–8)

1. How do you respond to the notion of seeing our lives as "trailers" for the bigger story of God's reign and rule? Does it strike you as intimidating? Arrogant? Energizing? Something else? Why?

2. What has been your experience of journaling? Do you find it helpful? Do you find it taxing? What about journaling might qualify it as a "spiritual practice"?

3. Which of the missional priorities—justice, beauty, wholeness—do you gravitate toward most? Which do you find particularly challenging to implement into your weekly rhythms? Why?

4. Do you find it difficult to understand yourself as a missionary? Why or why not? How have you seen your self-understanding change as you've begun to cultivate these habits in your life?

5. "It takes much longer than we have assumed" to form a habit—especially the kinds of habits discussed in this book. What have you found gets in your way as you try to develop new habits?

6. Which of the goals of the DNA triad—discipleship, nurture, accountability—is most appealing to you? Which sounds most intimidating? Why?

7. Who are some people who have been particularly supportive in your spiritual growth? What made them so significant to your faith life?

8. How has taking on the habits of journaling your missionary experience and of gathering for discipleship, nurture, and accountability shaped your faith lately? In what ways have these habits surprised your friends and neighbors?

9. Now that you've read this book and taken on these habits, what do you see as the next steps for you, your friends, and your church to take in order to more effectively surprise the world with the good news of the reign and rule of God?

APPENDIX
Resources for Learning Jesus

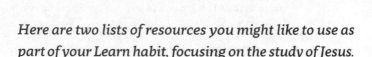

Here are two lists of resources you might like to use as part of your Learn habit, focusing on the study of Jesus.

GREAT BOOKS ABOUT JESUS

Philip Yancey. *The Jesus I Never Knew*. Grand Rapids, MI: Zondervan, 1995. Now a classic. Yancey uncovers a Jesus who is brilliant, creative, challenging, fearless, compassionate, unpredictable, and ultimately satisfying. A great read.

N. T. Wright. *The Challenge of Jesus*. Downers Grove, IL: IVP, 1999. A highly stimulating treatment of the hard, historical work needed to understand Jesus within the Palestinian world of the first century, as well as a passionate call to follow Jesus more faithfully into our world today.

J. John. *The Life: A Portrait of Jesus*. London: Authentic Media, 2003. An excellent introduction to the living, breathing human being at the center of the Christian good news: Jesus of Nazareth. Easy to read, with helpful answers to some of the common questions we all have about Jesus' life. Read it and then give it to your non-Christian friends.

Dave Roberts. *Following Jesus: A Non-Religious Guidebook for the Spiritually Hungry*. Orlando, FL: Relevant Books, 2004. This book will revolutionize your walk with God, revealing a perspective on Jesus you've never seen before. Explores what a real, dynamic relationship with Jesus looks like. Excellent, particularly if your faith life is getting a little stale.

Rob Bell. *Velvet Elvis: Repainting the Christian Faith*. Grand Rapids, MI: Zondervan, 2005. Looks at how Jesus wants to be reflected in church communities today. The well-researched Jewish background of Jesus is fascinating. Simple but profound.

John Dickson. *A Spectator's Guide to Jesus*. Oxford: Lion Hudson, 2005. The back cover sums it up: "If you have ever wondered how a crucified Palestinian peasant could end up winning the allegiance of 2 billion confessed Christians today, this book will provide some of the answers." Really useful historical teaching to correct some of the rubbish out there!

Don Everts. *God in the Flesh*. Downers Grove, IL: IVP Books, 2005. Looks at Jesus via the reactions of those who met him. The real Jesus jumps off the page and comes to life as a compelling person and very, very cool. Short studies included. Good for a personal devotion or maybe a home group discussion.

Conrad Gempf. *Mealtime Habits of the Messiah*. Grand Rapids, MI: Zondervan, 2005. A funny, quirky, and informative book that looks at forty of Jesus' encounters with others, with questions for reflection. Jesus: alive, fun, engaging, warm, and occasionally dangerous. This will give you an extra shot for the day.

Mike Erre. *The Jesus of Suburbia: Have We Tamed the Son of God to Fit Our Lifestyle?* Nashville: W Publishing, 2006. Have we settled for a watered-down, safe, comfortable Christianity? Mike Erre paints an exciting, inspiring, and powerful picture of the real Jesus. He challenges us to embrace the message of Jesus Christ as a revolutionary, life-transforming, culture-impacting movement of God. Brilliant! Good for firing you up for a radical life of sacrificial Jesus-following!

Tom Taylor. *Paradoxy: Coming to Grips with the Contradictions of Jesus*. Grand Rapids, MI: Baker, 2006. This book unfolds some of the core mysteries of Jesus' upside-down teachings (for example, die to live, serve to reign, and walk by faith not by sight). More than any other book, *Paradoxy* helped me understand the lifestyle Jesus wants his followers to live. Really explains why doing life Jesus' way is better than any other.

Kenneth Bailey. *Jesus Through Middle Eastern Eyes*. Downers Grove, IL: IVP Academic, 2008. At over four hundred pages, this very weighty exploration puts Jesus in his sociopolitical and religio-cultural context. Challenging, but essential reading for those wanting to understand Jesus.

GREAT FILMS ABOUT JESUS

The Gospel According to St. Matthew (1964). Directed by controversial Italian filmmaker Pier Paulo Pasolini, every single line of dialogue comes directly from Matthew's Gospel. Jesus wears a black hooded cloak and seems dangerous and radical. The film is gritty and down-to-earth, and it underscores the revolutionary nature of Christ's message. After viewing this you can understand why the authorities would want to crucify this guy.

Godspell (1973). Sure, it's a musical set in New York City (one sequence even takes place on the roofs of the then-brand-new World Trade Center), but it's a joyous meditation on the teachings of Jesus— especially the parables and the Sermon on the Mount—and how they resonated with the countercultural mood of that time. Controversial in its day, it helps us see the joy of Jesus and his vision for the world.

Jesus of Nazareth (1977). Not really a film but a six-hour miniseries directed by Franco Zeffirelli, this fleshes out the supporting characters in ways that convey the breadth and depth of the impact Jesus had on his contemporaries.

Jesus of Montreal (1989). A Canadian film about a troupe of actors who put on an unorthodox but acclaimed Passion play that incites the opposition of the Catholic Church. Daniel, the actor playing Christ, finds his life beginning to mirror that of the real Jesus. This is a clever retelling that highlights Jesus' opposition to organized religion.

The Passion of the Christ (2004). Mel Gibson's deeply personal film about the death of Christ was inspired not only by the Gospels but also by the stations of the Cross (a devotional practice built into the architecture of most Catholic churches) and the visions of Sister Anne Catherine Emmerich, a stigmatic German nun. Its stark, gruesome depiction of the suffering of Christ is unforgettable. More than any recent director, Gibson captures the grand supernatural conflict which gives the death of Christ its meaning.

The Chronicles of Narnia: The Lion, the Witch and the Wardrobe (2005). Like *Jesus of Montreal*, this isn't a film about Jesus himself, but it presents one of the most beautiful Jesus-like figures in popular culture: the wild but good Aslan, king of Narnia.

The Nativity Story (2006). While it includes inaccuracies like the Wise Men appearing in Bethlehem at the time of Jesus' birth and bends the biblical accounts a bit here and there, this is nonetheless a powerful depiction of simple, beautiful faith, the love of family, and the strange ways that God moves.

NOTES

INTRODUCTION

1. Felicity Dale, *An Army of Ordinary People* (Carol Stream, IL: Tyndale House, 2010).

CHAPTER ONE—LIVING "QUESTIONABLE" LIVES

1. John Dickson, *The Best Kept Secret of Christian Mission* (Grand Rapids, MI: Zondervan, 2010), p. 93.
2. Dickson, *Best Kept Secret*, p. 94.

CHAPTER TWO—A NEW SET OF HABITS

1. David Bosch, *Believing in the Future* (Harrisburg, PA: Trinity Press International, 1995), p. 33.
2. John P. Kotter and Dan S. Cohen, *The Heart of Change* (Boston: Harvard Business School Press, 2002).
3. Lee Beach, *The Church in Exile* (Downers Grove, IL: IVP Academic, 2015), p. 203.

CHAPTER THREE—BLESS: THE FIRST HABIT

1. Gary Chapman, *The Five Love Languages* (Chicago: Northfield Publishing, 2010), p. 46.

2. Dave Ferguson, *Discover Your Mission Now*, Exponential eBook Series, https://www.exponential.org/ebooks/discovermission/.
3. Jomo Kenyatta, reported in John Frederick Walker, *A Certain Curve of Horn: The Hundred-Year Quest for the Giant Sable Antelope of Angola* (New York: Grove Press, 2004), p. 144; also attributed to Archbishop Desmond Tutu.

CHAPTER FOUR—EAT: THE SECOND HABIT

1. "Pliny the Younger and Trajan on the Christians," *Early Christian Writings*, http://www.earlychristianwritings.com/text/pliny.html.
2. Janice Price, with the World Mission and Anglican Communion Panel, *World-Shaped Mission: Reimagining Mission Today* (London: Church House Publishing, 2012), p. 24.
3. Simon Carey Holt, *Eating Heaven: Spirituality at the Table* (Moreland, Australia: Acorn Press, 2013), p. 150.
4. Alan Hirsch and Lance Ford, *Right Here, Right Now* (Grand Rapids, MI: Baker Books, 2011), p. 203.
5. Ben F. Meyer, *The Aims of Jesus* (London: SCM Press, 1979), p. 161.

CHAPTER FIVE—LISTEN: THE THIRD HABIT

1. Bruce Demarest, *Satisfy Your Soul* (Colorado Springs: NavPress, 1999), p. 133.
2. Dietrich Bonhoeffer, quoted in Dale Larsen and Sandy Larsen, *Dietrich Bonhoeffer: Costly Grace* (Downers Grove, IL: InterVarsity Press, 2002), p. 44.
3. Thomas Merton, *A Year with Thomas Merton*, ed. Jonathan Montaldo (New York: HarperCollins, 2004), p. 8.
4. Joshua Searle and Roy Searle, "Monastic Practices and the *Missio Dei*," *Journal of Missional Practice* 3 (Fall 2013), http://journalof missionalpractice.com/index.php/issue-3/monastic-practices-and -the-missio-dei#_ednref17.
5. Thérèse of Lisieux, quoted in Heather King, "St. Thérèse of Lisieux's Christmas Eve Conversion," December 18, 2014, http://angelusnews.

com/entertainment/culture/st-therese-of-lisieuxs-christmas-eve
-conversion-7092/#.VJhuOF5CAA.

6. Thomas Merton, *Contemplative Prayer* (New York: Image Classics, 1971), p. 19.

7. Phil Fox Rose, "Meditation for Christians," *On the Way*, http://www.patheos.com/blogs/philfoxrose/meditation-for-christians/.

CHAPTER SIX—LEARN: THE FOURTH HABIT

1. C. S. Lewis, *Mere Christianity* (New York, Simon & Schuster Touchstone, 1996), p. 171.

2. John Stackhouse, *Need to Know: Vocation as the Heart of Christian Epistemology* (Oxford: Oxford University Press, 2014), p. 63.

3. Ross Langmead, *Word Made Flesh: Towards an Incarnational Missiology* (Lanham, MD: University Press of America, 2004), p. 219.

4. Stackhouse, *Need to Know*, pp. 62–63.

5. Stackhouse, *Need to Know*, p. 63.

6. Michael Frost, *Jesus the Fool* (Grand Rapids, MI: Baker, 2010).

7. Michael Frost and Alan Hirsch, *ReJesus: A Wild Messiah for a Missional Church* (Grand Rapids, MI: Baker, 2009).

8. N. T. Wright, *The Challenge of Jesus: Rediscovering Who Jesus Was and Is* (Downers Grove, IL: InterVarsity Press, 1999); Darrell Bock, *Jesus According to Scripture: Restoring the Portrait from the Gospels* (Grand Rapids, MI: Baker, 2002); Craig Blomberg, *Jesus and the Gospels* (Nashville: B&H Academic, 1997); Tim Keller, *King's Cross: The Story of the World in the Life of Jesus* (New York: Dutton, 2011).

CHAPTER SEVEN—SENT: THE FIFTH HABIT

1. Michael Frost, *The Road to Missional* (Grand Rapids, MI: Baker, 2011), p. 29.

2. Frost, *Road to Missional*, pp. 104–112.

3. C. S. Lewis, *C. S. Lewis: Readings for Meditation and Reflection* (New York City: HarperOne, 1996), p. 93.

4. Anne Broyles, *Journaling: A Spiritual Journey* (Nashville: Upper Room, 1999), p. 10.

CHAPTER EIGHT—DISCIPLESHIP, NURTURE, AND ACCOUNTABILITY

1. Rick Warren, *Forty Days of Purpose* (Lake Forest, CA: Saddleback Church, 2002), a church campaign associated with the book *The Purpose-Driven Life*.
2. Jeremy Dean, *Making Habits, Breaking Habits: Why We Do Things, Why We Don't, and How to Make Any Change Stick* (Boston: De Capo Press, 2013), p. 6.
3. For more on Life Transformation Groups, see http://www.cmaresources.org/article/ltg.

ABOUT THE AUTHOR

Michael Frost is an internationally recognized missiologist and one of the leading voices in the missional-church movement. His books are required reading in colleges and seminaries around the world, and he is much sought after as an international conference speaker. Frost is the vice principal of Morling College, the founding director of the Tinsley Institute, the founding pastor of Small Boat Big Sea, and cofounder of the Forge International Mission Training Network. His books include *The Shaping of Things to Come*, *Exiles*, and *Incarnate*.

YOU HAVE NEIGHBORS. YOU'RE IN RELATIONSHIPS.
——— YOU LIVE SOMEWHERE. ———

WHAT IF YOU STAYED?

#stayingisthenewgoing
#stayforth

SURPRISE
YOUR CHURCH!

Together, learn how to share your faith in surprisingly simple ways. The BELLS model is an easy, effective way for your whole church to develop simple habits in order to live and share the gospel. Use it as part of your next teaching series, in evangelism training, or as a small-group study.